Ascension 101

A Roadmap for Your Soul

Kimberly Palm

Important Caution:

This publication contains the opinions and ideas of the author and is sold with the understanding that neither the author or the publisher are engaged in rendering medical, health, psychological, or any other kind of personal or professional services in the book. Nor is anything in this book intended to be a diagnosis, prescription, or cure for any specific kind of medical or psychological or emotional problems. If the reader requires medical, health, or other assistance or advice, a competent professional should be consulted.

The author and publisher specifically disclaim all responsibility for any liability, loss or risk, personal or otherwise, that is incurred as a consequence, directly or indirectly, of the use and application of the contents of this book.

Cover design by Kimberly Palm
Edited by: Peter Messerschmidt
Foreward by: Rev. Sarah Nash

ISBN: 978-0-9973252-2-5
Ebook ISBN: 978-0-9973252-3-2

This book is dedicated to the God of Unconditional Love, Yeshua, Mary Magdalene, Mother Mary and to all humans seeking the light and the truth.

Table of Contents

Foreward

When Kimberly told me that she had been approached by her sources of illumination with the request that she present a "Fuller Package" for this era in the form of the book you're about to read; I knew that much of the world was truly "waking up".

This important and timely message about Ascension, or as I call it: enlightenment, is written by one of the clearest and purest channels I have had the opportunity to collaborate with. Many of the philosophies, suggestions, and information outlined in the following pages are rich with the countless hours of discussions we shared in the course of the last decade.

This process of "Ascension" is not about dying and lifting your soul to a perfect place. That is reserved for a separate element of the unique process of life after death. The better question here is, *"How do I prepare my inner being to accept more fully the consciousness I feel I deserve now?"*

Keep in mind that most traditional dogma prevents or possibly even forbids that question. Kimberly reminds us again and again that this is the doorway to her promotion of "Ascension". There is no key or special rule. Everything is yours, already.

My personal ministry has been dedicated to the power of positive focused intention through prayer and meditation. Lift yourself out of the common realm and into the uncommon realm of individual accountability through experiencing a Greater Source of Love with your inner guide. I encourage each gentle reader to set aside the limiting beliefs keeping you in the darkness of shame and guilt. Simply being open to the *possibility* is enough, for now.

I keep a quote on my desktop to remind me. From "I Am That: Talks with Sri Nisargadatta Maharaj:"

> "All you need is already within you, only you must approach yourself with reverence and love. Self-condemnation and self-distrust are grievous errors. Your constant flight from pain and search for pleasure is a sign of love you bear for yourself, all I plead with you is this: make love of yourself perfect. Deny yourself nothing -- give yourself infinity and eternity and discover that you do not need them; you are beyond."
> — Sri Nisargadatta Maharaj

Many of the answers to *"where do I go now that my eyes are opened?"* can be decided by following this "road map to your soul." This is, by no means, a perfect roadmap either. Kimberly will tell you that she can only work with the limited information that a good and benevolent source has given her. It is up to you to figure out how to manage the detours, and the roadblocks. It is not easy, but it is worth the journey.

I will finish with a final cliché: Do not forget to stop and look around you from time to time. That is all part of the fun too. Wherever you are, there you are.

> — *Reverend Sarah Nash,*
> *Founder of The*
> *White Light Express*
> *September 2020*

Introduction

This book was written for any person who is a spiritual seeker, looking for information to assist them on their spiritual journey. Whether you are a newly awakened seeker of the truth, a spiritually enlightened person, a lightworker or an accomplished spiritual teacher, this book offers something for anyone seeking the truth, the light, and the way.

This book is not about religion, doctrine or cults. I respect everyone's religion, personal journey, beliefs, and way to the truth. If you read this book and realize that it does not resonate with you or determine that you do not like my beliefs and opinions, that is okay. I am not here to convince you to adopt my belief system.

I am simply here to authentically stand in my own truth and share information I have channeled, along with information that comes from my personal knowledge in order to assist people with their Ascension. You need to find your own beliefs and experience your own personal journey. However, if you do agree with the essence of my book and my words resonate with you, then I am honored to be of service to you.

I wrote this book for two reasons.

First, I have been channeling Yeshua (Christ) for many years and it was he who asked me to write this book to help him continue spreading the message he was teaching while he was walking the Earth.

Most of this book was essentially written by him, since a huge portion of it came to me through channeled messages. All of Yeshua's messages that have been channeled through me over the years have been positive, uplifting, loving, eye opening, accurate and very educational.

Second, I noticed ever increasing numbers of people in spiritual groups on social media asking many of the questions I have answered by this book, including many variations of "Who and what is God?" "What is my purpose?" along with numerous other spiritual and esoteric questions.

When Yeshua first requested that I write this book, I asked him what to name the book. He gave me the first part of the title and explained to me that part of the reason I am here on Earth right now, is to help those people who are ready with their Ascension. Hence the first part of the title.

The reason this book is subtitled *"A Roadmap for your Soul"*, is that every soul has the same final destination, which is a rejoining or reunion with the Creative Source that made everything, including your divine spirit.

However, each and every one of us will take a different path or road to get to that final destination. We will all use a different mode of transportation to get there and we will take our own time to get there. Life is not a competition, nor does it have a deadline. You have all the time you need to get to your own final destination of enlightenment, and eventual return to Divine Source Creator of Everything.

This book provides you with a roadmap to get to your final soul destination. You and only you can determine which road or roads you will choose, how long you will take and what type of transportation you will use. Nobody can do that for you. It is up to you to discern and decide how you experience your own unique personal journey.

There are many people on this planet who call themselves a *"Guru."*

You do not need a Guru for your spiritual enlightenment and growth. I am not a Guru to anyone and will never call myself a Guru. I am a spiritual teacher and mentor and I provide you and my clients with guidance, tools and information to help you become your own Guru. Guru essentially means, "Gee, You are You". You already have all you need within yourself to find your own spiritual answers and find your own way down your road to Enlightenment. All you need is information, a little training, some tools, guidance and emotional support from teachers like me, friends and family.

You should not have to make a huge financial investment to experience spiritual growth. This book will give you some important basic tools and answers to many of your fundamental spiritual questions. You may also get answers to ideas you never thought of previously that will change your direction altogether and elevate you to levels you never dreamed of before.

There are thousands of pages of spiritual information I could have put into this book, but I chose not to because it would take me many years and I needed to get this information out right away to help people with the big event that has begun. However, I believe I covered most of the essential basic Ascension information you need to know. If you have questions after reading this book, I am happy to answer them in a private spiritual guidance session. My hope for you, is that when you finish this book, you will have learned at least a few new ideas to help you on your road to enlightenment and spiritual growth.

May you be blessed with love, light and peace always on your journey!

Chapter 1

What is Ascension and Why is it Important for Us?

Ascension: Definition according to the Oxford Dictionary

Ascension
[əˈsen(t)SH(ə)n]
NOUN
The act of rising to an important position or a higher level.
"his ascension to the ranks of pop star"

The ascent of Christ into heaven on the fortieth day after the Resurrection. synonyms:
rise · upward movement · takeoff · liftoff · launch · blastoff · climb · levitation · soaring · jump · leap

Ascension: Short definition for this book

Ascension is the process of spiritual awakening that moves a person from one level of consciousness into a higher level of consciousness. In the case of Earth, you are moving from a 3rd dimensional consciousness to a 5th dimensional consciousness. Ascension is knowing you have your "own" truth instead of the one that has been given to you by other people, systems, religions, schools, media and society and exploring that truth without any limitations or fear. It is taking back your own power, sovereignty and authority from other people and systems and no longer allowing anyone or anything to control you. As you ascend you are also stepping into full accountability for everything that you do, think, or say from this point forward.

Ascension: A more complex definition and description

The more complex explanation is that Ascension is basically an energetic frequency shift, spiritual shift, mental/emotional shift and physical shift all occurring concurrently.

Everything ever created is made of energy and vibrates at a specific frequency. As you ascend you are shedding all the old fear-based belief systems, programming and information that has been woven into society for thousands of years. You are leaving behind the ego, becoming more enlightened, and reprogramming your consciousness and DNA with a new love-based paradigm.

You are also bringing layers of light into your spiritual body and anchoring them into your physical plane of reality. Your energetic frequency is changing, and you are continuously uploading light codes that are activating your DNA and bio-energy field, as well as that of the planet. All humans and the planet Earth have been stuck in a low vibration, fear based, 3rd dimensional field and now we are going through a massive shift as a collective consciousness to a higher vibration, love based 5th dimension.

Ascension is not just something you are experiencing as an individual human. The entire planet is going through the Ascension process right now and as the DNA of Gaia Earth is upgraded to the new 5th dimension love based frequencies, *your* DNA is also shifting and changing on a daily basis to match the changes of the Earth. The children being born at this moment already have their DNA changed to match the frequencies we adults are all trying to reach. In order to have a positive upgrade experience, it is imperative that we keep our thoughts, behaviors and choices all positive. Each time the energy frequencies change on Earth, our bodies adjust. Later in this book, I will explain how to know that your body is adjusting.

As you go through the process of Ascension you will move from a place of separation from God and everyone else, to a feeling of interconnectedness and unity. Ascension is a massive transformation and transmutation process that is part of the human soul's journey within a cycle of evolutionary time. As we each go through this process, we leave behind old beliefs that have been around for thousands of years, concerning who we are, what we are, where we are going, what reality is and what life is really about. This means everything that makes up your body, mind, spirit and consciousness is being restructured into something new as a result of a vast inner transformation. In order to keep up with all the new frequencies streaming into the planet, we need to keep our body, mind and spirit vibration really high. Later in this book I will be telling you how to do that.

Some people believe that in order to Ascend you must die first. Keep in mind that there are many definitions of the word Ascension and the type of Ascension that requires dying is just one of them. However, that definition is not what we are covering in this book. We are discussing a different type of Ascension that our souls are all part of right now, in our human bodies while we are here in this lifetime on Earth. We are all participating in this process together. It is something we all chose to do a long time ago as a collective along with our mother Gaia (Earth) that we live on.

One of the main themes of this Ascension, is the liberation of humanity. Our planet has been in a type of lockdown for thousands of years. We have been stuck in this 3D reality with negative forces controlling the planet and keeping us all in a state of fear, control, and suffering. We — as a collective of souls — all allowed this to happen, initially for our learning purposes and an experimental classroom of sorts.

However, over time some negative demonic beings and entities came to Earth and took control of our situation and have subsequently kept us trapped in a matrix of fear and suffering for thousands of years. Part of our Ascension is liberation from this fear and suffering and our moving into a New Shamballa (Kingdom of Peace). We will have much more heaven on Earth very soon. Our creator who made our souls, loves us and wants us to be happy, healthy and live in joy, peace and unity.

Unfortunately, we have been "hijacked" and kept in a prison of suffering for a long time. It is very similar to passages in the Holy Bible, where we read about about Satan trying to destroy humans because we are God's creation. Satan and demonic entities have been the cause of all our illness, fear, suffering, starvation, wars, hate, grief and sorrow for a long time. Benevolent compassionate star beings and angelic beings are here now and have removed the lockdown matrix around our planet so we can complete our Ascension.

Our human brains have been controlled by an artificial intelligence program that has kept us locked in a pervasive pattern of false beliefs, fear, negativity, hatred and other negative mind patterns that were never beneficial for us. All this A.I. programming has now been removed, and for the first time in thousands of years we have our free will fully returned to us.

A major event will happen that will complete this cycle of Ascension for our planet. Many ancient cultures and indigenous tribes have predicted this event for thousands of years. They have also predicted the rise of the Rainbow Warriors, also known as the 144,000 light-warriors who are here now to help usher in this New Earth, Great Awakening and Era of Peace. I am grateful to be one of them. If you are reading this book, you may also be one of them. If you are not a lightworker, you are most likely a Starseed. Starseeds are beings from all over the Universe who have come to Earth and incarnated into human bodies to go through this Ascension process right now.

As we all go through this process every human has a choice to stay in low density 3D or to ascend to 5D and even higher consciousness levels. It is important to know that you do not need to be awake or spiritual to Ascend in this body now. In order to Ascend, you simply need to be at least 60% (or more) loving, kind, compassionate, and a person who focuses mostly on service to others. You could even be totally asleep but be love based (heart centered) and service to others based and you will still be able to Ascend while in your current body, in this lifetime.

However, those people who are fear based and mostly focused on service to self, and who make a conscious choice to stay that way will not Ascend on Earth in their current body. They will be given other opportunities to Ascend in future lifetimes on other planets. As Earth moves into the higher frequencies and becomes a 5th density planet, the people who remain stuck in a 3D reality and who refuse to change will not be able to stay here because they will not be able to handle the higher energies. Many of them will leave via death or be taken off the planet.

There are many adults and children who are high vibrational, positive, loving and service to others oriented who are not awake. Do not worry about these people coming with you into the New Earth reality. They are safe and protected and will be there with us. I had to ask Yeshua about this information, because my own family members are not awake or spiritual and I was concerned about them not being able to stay with me in the New Earth we are creating.

It is also important to know, that there are many reasons why your friends and family who are high vibrational are still asleep. For some it may have to do with their career, for others it may have to do with their life contract and then there are additional other possible reasons. The reasons do not matter as much as simply understanding that high vibrational loving humans do not have to be awakened or spiritual in order to Ascend. However, if you have family members or friends who are low vibration, fear based, not loving, are mostly of a service-to-self orientation, and who are not wanting to change, they will not be coming with you. Many of us have at least *one* family member who is like this and despite our loving them, they do not choose to love or to change. Do not fear for them or be sad for them, because they are on their own soul evolution time schedule that does not match up with yours. Eventually they will come to the light.

Everyone on this planet is encoded with triggers designed to activate celestial knowledge and memories of who we really are, where we came from and more, when our conscious awareness reaches certain levels of awakening. It has been predicted that when we Ascend fully to 5D, we will have all sorts of new abilities including psychic abilities, telepathy, channeling, clairvoyance, clairsentience, clairaudience, prophesy, levitation, instant manifestation, speaking light language and other new languages, and much more. These abilities are similar to what you have when you are in heaven.

The process we are currently going through is being escalated at a fast pace to prevent humanity from going through another mass extinction event. This planet has gone through several mass extinctions due to our past failures, along with the influence of the negative entities who have been controlling Earth for a long time. We have currently entered the 6th mass extinction phase. With over 200 species going extinct daily, the current rate of destruction is unprecedented in Earth's history and we are running out of time. We are experiencing an out-of-control domino effect with radical loss of insect species, as well as birds, amphibians and other animals. There is also a series of events happening that are a repeat of events that led up to the destruction of Lemuria and Atlantis thousands of years ago. These events are all being orchestrated by the dark entities who have been controlling the planet. It is their last-ditch effort to destroy humanity and Gaia. As people are waking up everywhere on the planet, these entities are losing their foothold and becoming desperate. Most of the people on this planet will have to wake up quickly and make drastic changes if we are to save our Earth.

The awakening of humanity is happening right now in exponential rates. Before the Covid19 pandemic in January 2020, the number of people awake on the planet was at approximately 3%. As I write this book in May of 2020 the number of awake people on the planet is at close to 9%.

We all chose to incarnate into our bodies at this exact time for the "Great Awakening". This event has been prophesized by all of the indigenous cultures throughout history. The Holy Bible mentions the "Great Awakening" in the book of Revelations. The word Apocalypse actually means "lifting of the veil" or "revealing". It has to do with disclosing the truth that has been hidden from humanity. Humanity has been put under a sleep spell for thousands of years. A veil has been in place that separated us from the truth of who we really are. This veil also separated us from each other so many people could not see how we are all connected. The veil of disconnection, ignorance and cultural manipulation has been a driving force of racism on the planet. We have had our divinity removed and we have been separated from our Creator God. Yeshua, who is also known as the Christ, came here to help tear down the veil that has been keeping you from the truth of who you really are. Other Ascended masters came before him and tried to do the same. All the three major patriarchal religions have created an illusion of duality; that you and I are separate from God and each other.

As I already mentioned, the Earth has been stuck in this 3rd dimensional fear-based energy cycle for thousands of years. Dark malevolent forces have been controlling the Earth for a long time and kept us stuck in something that is similar to the A.I. matrix in the movie "The Matrix."

The dark forces in control have imposed a patriarchal low vibrational energy that keeps humans stuck in a state of fear and suffering. Part of how they have done this is by stripping away the sacred feminine divinity that is sometimes called the Sophia or divine feminine Christ Consciousness. These are the feminine aspects of God which keep souls anchored in a place of heart centered love instead of the masculine energies of fear that have dominated the Earth for too long.

Some of these malevolent forces included our history's religious leaders who have enslaved us with a mass patriarchy and turned females into 2nd class citizens. This began with the biblical stories of the 1st woman Eve being evil and working with Satan to get knowledge.

Women have been demonized all throughout history as witches and worse, and prevented from being leaders, speakers, healers, teachers and holding important positions in society.

These dark forces have kept humanity in a sleep spell in order to enslave us and take away our knowledge of who we really are and our connection to Source Creator. They have removed our divinity Christ talked about. They have been feeding on our fear and suffering and have created banking and financial systems designed to keep us trapped in despair and enslavement. They have also perpetuated non-stop hate, racism, violence and wars worldwide. We have been trapped in a system of slavery without even knowing it, while all along believing that we have freedom. That freedom has been false. They have used many things like fluoride, poisoned foods, chemtrails, movies, television, advertising, cults and lies about our history to dumb down and enslave humanity so that we cannot access direct connection with our higher selves and God. They have created a world where humans cannot think for themselves and need the world governments to make decisions for them. Instead of depending on and turning to God and spirit, they have tricked humans into turning away from God and spirit and focusing on the material world, wealth and fame.

There should always be a balance of both feminine and masculine energy on this planet; the yin and the yang. Preferably there should be more feminine than masculine, 60% or 70% feminine and 30% or 40% masculine energy. The reason for the emphasis on the feminine is that it is the nurturing and loving energy. However, in recent times the masculine energy on Earth has been around 95% and feminine energy only 5%, which is why we need more love in this world.

For those of you who do not know, feminine energy is heart based, loving and compassionate. Feminine energy is sometimes referred to as Sophia energy, Mother Mary energy, Quan Yin energy or Mary Magdalene energy because the side of God and the feminine Christed masters were focused on love and compassion. The divine feminine side of God is known in Gnostic Christianity and Ancient Judaism as Sophia. In Buddhism the feminine side of the Buddha is known as Green Tara. Tara is also called Dolma by the Tibetans and is commonly thought to be a Bodhisattva or Buddha of compassion and action. She is a protector who comes to our aid to relieve us of physical, emotional and spiritual suffering.

If you are wondering why we live on this Earth with evil or dark forces that control everything, you need to understand the Law of Opposites and the fact that this is Classroom Earth. It is a great experiment. I was originally going to name this book *"Classroom Earth – Making the Grade"*. The reason being that we are here for this Great Awakening, but we are also here to learn. Earth is a giant classroom and you are the student. Even though I am a spiritual teacher in this life, I am also a student and I will always be learning new lessons.

In order for us to learn, we need to have the "Law of Opposites". This means that there has to be positive and negative, black and white, day and night, dark and light, good and evil. If everything was perfect and good and love and light, then we would not have left our real home of heaven to come here, because this would already *be* heaven. Many of us have been here in many lifetimes and we are all here now for the purpose of the Great Awakening, ushering in the New Earth and to learn lessons that we have all chosen to learn. According to what the Ascended masters are telling lightworkers right now, this new Ascended Earth and our new Ascended bodies will be experiencing all sorts of wonderful things.

We will enter what people are calling "The Golden Age". We will have psychic powers and other abilities we have never had before. We will have our memories of past lifetimes restored and we will even be able to speak telepathically.

If you are reading this book, it is because you and I are here now to restore peace, love, compassion and balance to our planet. There are no coincidences and you have made a choice to read this book now.

As your soul grows spiritually and Ascends, you go through many dimensional layers or densities that range from 1D to 7D. There are even higher densities or dimensions beyond the 7th level where different types of beings like angels exist. We are all here right now for the "Great Awakening" and to raise the consciousness of the planet from 3D fear-based consciousness to 5D love-based consciousness. In the future our planetary consciousness will also have the opportunity to rise to the 6th and 7th dimension.

Most of the people on Earth reside in 3rd density. As we each go up through these levels of consciousness, we may be in a single level at a time or sometimes we can partially exist in two or more levels at the same time. Please keep in mind that I am not judging anyone by their level of consciousness because we are all on our own unique journey that we travel in our own time. Awakening and Ascension is not a contest or competition. I have met several newly awakened people who compare themselves to other spiritual people and they are upset that they are not successful at using crystals, meditating, or they don't have psychic powers yet. Everyone's experience on this Earth and beyond is unique and all soul journeys are unique. As you read through this information please be compassionate with yourself and do not judge yourself. The fact that you are reading these words now, means that you are on your way, in a very positive direction, so be kind to yourself as your spirit advances on your journey.

Description of people who are in 3rd Density consciousness

The humans in 3rd density consciousness possess at least several — or potentially all — of the following attributes:

- They are egocentric and self-serving.
- They are fear based; their behaviors and actions are based on fear instead of love.
- They only give conditional love, meaning they only love you if you do something for them or serve them somehow. If you do not meet their expectations, they do not love you.
- They have a lack of compassion.
- These people judge others and they judge themselves.
- They are competitive and self-righteous.
- They tend to be racists.
- They are not conscious of other people around them and do not care.
- They lack consciousness in general.
- They focus on blaming and shaming themselves and others.
- They have total lack of respect for themselves and other people and animals.
- They purposefully do harm to other humans or to animals.
- They harm themselves in many ways, typically including abusing their bodies, addictions, prostitution, etc.
- They do not care for the Earth and do not feel remorse about destroying the Earth.

- They can be self-destructive or destroy other people and things.
- They identify with their physical body instead of their soul.
- They tend to be jealous, possessive, narcissistic and mean.
- They are not accountable for their actions.
- They have a feeling of self-importance and think they are better than others.
- They live in a world of scarcity.
- They do not trust people and may not trust themselves.
- They are in a constant mode of flight or fight.
- These people are very materialistic.
- They place more emphasis on money and possessions than they do on relationships and other things that are much more important.
- They are emotionally charged by past and future and they are always reactive.

Description of people who are in 4th Density consciousness

If you are reading this book you are most likely primarily in 4th dimension or you may even be in 5th dimension consciousness. Some of you might still have little remnants of 3rd that you are working on and that is okay. Like I said before we are all on different journeys in our own time.

In 4th dimensional consciousness you transition from the Egoic fear-based reality to one of love. A spiritual awakening starts to happen, and you start to expand your consciousness. You develop lots of spiritual questions and you begin to purge your negative emotions and false belief systems. Instead of focusing on your physical body only, you start to realize that you are not a physical body but a divine spirit living in a physical body.

Many physical changes can happen to you. You will begin to tap into the collective consciousness. The most exciting part is that you will start to develop special abilities and have interesting paranormal experiences, including the following:

- You may start to see spirits or ghosts.
- You may experience pre-cognition or telepathy.
- You could have out of body or astral travel experiences.
- You may see and feel energy.
- You may develop clairaudience or other clair-related gifts.
- You begin to realize that the world is changing around you.
- You may start communicating with your guides and angels or E.T.s and other types of beings.
- Service to others becomes important to you and you learn how to manifest.

In general, 4th Density humans see the importance of taking care of their bodies (temple of the Holy Spirit). They also see the importance of taking care of other people, animals and of the Earth.

Description of people who are in 5th Density consciousness

When your consciousness arrives in 5th density consciousness you become totally egoless and embody most — if not all — of the following attributes:

- Your main focus becomes on being of service to others.
- All your actions are based on love and you are in a state of unconditional love.
- Gratitude becomes a daily practice.
- Compassion and forgiveness become part of who you are.
- You become completely self-realized.
- You know who you really are and why you are here.
- You may have remembrance of many or all past lifetimes.
- You also realize that you are limitless.
- Your physical body becomes less dense.
- You feel like a big weight has been removed from you.
- You develop a unity mind and recognize yourself as part of the whole.
- Manifestation is easy for you as you are constantly co-creating with Source.
- Instead of struggling like you used to, you just go with the flow of life.
- Duality and linear time dissolves.
- You really feel your timelessness.
- You have no need for status or possessions.
- You place all importance in your life on non-tangible things like relationships, love, service and education, instead of the 3D focus on materialism.
- You are able to travel astrally and you develop many psychic gifts.
- You live every day with purpose, and you have a close connection with Creator God, all humans, all animals and all of creation.

There are many other attributes to these dimensions or densities, but I want to avoid giving you a brain overload. Can you recognize yourself in these descriptions? If so, then you will know where you are headed next. We all are here to move humanity into a 5th dimensional consciousness and create heaven on Earth.

I wrote these words during the Covid-19 crisis in 2020, because Yeshua asked me to write this book. Much of the information in this book was channeled, but I also had Yeshua pop into the room and speak to me from time to time. I have been able to hear his audible voice for many years as he has given me important messages, both for myself and for humanity. One time when he popped in, he showed me a visual "movie" of when he resurrected Lazarus from the dead. He said to me, *Kimberly the world you have known is about to die and I am going to resurrect a New Shamballa.*"

I had no clue what the word "Shamballa" meant and had to look it up. It means "Kingdom of Peace". At a different time Yeshua popped in and told me, *Very soon there will be much more heaven on Earth*". He recently popped in again when I was asking about what will happen to all the evil people on the planet (people who commit crimes against humanity). His answer was that the Meek will inherit the earth and the evil ones will all be leaving. This is the reverse of what is mentioned in the book of revelations in the Bible with Christians and Jews being taken off the planet first. What I do know is that time on the other side in heaven and other dimensions is different than our time here.

One thing that many spiritual people — along with the indigenous peoples — know is that our Mother Earth is a conscious sentient being. She is alive and she has a consciousness. One of the many reasons I came to Earth at this time, in this body, is to support Gaia with the love and compassion she needs right now to make it through the big changes that are happening.

Gaia is a compassionate being and has been locked into a prison matrix grid for a very long time and she wants her freedom. She is tired of all the discarnate and negative energies and beings that have infiltrated her and have been working hard to destroy her for thousands of years. She is ready for a huge change. A while back, she sent out an SOS to the Universe asking for help. The angel armies and benevolent extraterrestrials are here now to help Gaia and to help us. Also, I chose to come here at this time to help her.

If you are a starseed, indigo or lightworker, you also chose to come here and help our Mother Gaia to transform, and to rid herself of the dark energies that have been here for too long. According to most spiritual people, indigenous tribes and lightworkers, this massive ascension process really began in 2012. The previous Atlantean Golden Age ended in 2012 and coincided with the completion of a 5,126-year cycle on the Mayan calendar on December 21, 2012.

At that moment, we officially began the next 26,000-year cycle and our world started heading towards its Ascension. This is the first time in history that a huge number of souls have come to Earth from all over space and time and incarnated themselves in human bodies just for the Great Awakening and transformation of Earth. If you have watched any videos or read any books by Dolores Cannon, she talks extensively about these concepts.

While you and I are going through this Earth Ascension, we are feeling certain side effects and symptoms. This is because Mother Gaia (Earth) is getting a huge DNA upgrade and so are we. Every time she upgrades, every living thing on the planet does, as well.

I would like to cover some of the symptoms with you so that you are able to discern when you are experiencing Ascension symptoms. Please keep in mind that I am not a doctor and if you have any significant health issues it is important for you to see a doctor to be diagnosed or to rule out anything physiologically serious.

If you go to doctors and they shake their heads and cannot diagnose you, or discount you and send you on your way without answers, chances are you may be experiencing Ascension symptoms.

If you are having many of the symptoms on this list, all at the same time, it is very likely related to Ascension. Keep in mind that not *all* the symptoms on my list may be due to the Ascension process. Please follow your own inner guidance. If you are having Ascension symptoms, please be loving and compassionate with yourself. Give yourself lots of self-care and remember that it is good to use natural and holistic remedies to heal. You can also go to a really good medical intuitive, who can help you determine the difference between real health issues and Ascension symptoms.

The following is a list of some of the negative Ascension symptoms I — and other people I know — have experienced in the course of the past several years. I have personally noticed these symptoms starting around 2011. Other people may have noticed them starting earlier or later.

- Dizziness.
- Headaches.
- Feeling stuffy headed; head pressure or like your head is being squeezed; head or face tingles or has feeling of "pins and needles."

- Sinus pressure even if you don't have allergies or a real cold.
- Blurry vision.
- Digestive problems.
- Heart palpitations.
- Feeling tired, drained, fatigue or low energy for no reason.
- Extreme sensitivities to your environment.
- New allergies or increase in allergies.
- Mystery illnesses.
- Problems sleeping, or waking up at weird times like 3 AM, 4 AM, 12 AM.
- Phantom pain.
- Feeling overwhelmed or anxious.
- Dark night of the soul.
- Sudden memory problems, absentmindedness not caused by illness, drugs, or genetics.
- Scattered thinking or confusion, brain fog or brain freezes, being tongue-tied often, or scattered thinking.
- Feeling suddenly hyperactive, with no apparent cause.
- Emotional extremes or heightened emotions. Feeling angry for no reason, feeling sad for no reason. Right now, during Ascension everyone's emotions are bubbling up to the surface to be released. A lot of repressed and subconscious fears, grief, anger, unforgiveness, sadness, rejection and past hurts are all coming up to be released.
- Sudden or extreme changes in body temperature, circulatory issues, sudden increased sensitivity or intolerance to heat or cold, circulation issues, having chills or feelings of being cold all the time without reason, or periods of feeling extremely warm, hot flashes, night sweats and waves of heat

throughout the body or in certain areas when you are not a menopausal woman.

- Sudden nervous feelings like you are jumping out of your skin.
- Inability to be around lots of people without feeling drained.
- Extreme sensitivity to cell phones, computers and other electrical devices.
- Extreme sensitivity to certain sounds or smells.
- Hearing high frequency sound or ringing in ears.
- Out of body experiences.
- Multi-dimensional experiences (can be both good and bad).
- Astral travel (can be both good and bad).
- Nightmares, intense, wild or bizarre dreams, lucid dreams, dreaming of people who have passed away.
- Feeling like you have time traveled.
- Seeing weird flashes of light, colors or orbs whether your eyes are open *or* closed. Seeing auras around objects, plants, trees, animals or people.
- Having electrical or battery run appliances and devices act strange around you, malfunctioning when you touch them or shutting off without reason, especially when in a state of high vibration or heightened emotions. Depleting batteries quickly.
- Noticing time shifts, Mandela effect, time seems to fly by much quicker than ever before, feeling like time is running out.
- Constant feeling like something big is about to happen but you don't know what and you need to prepare for it.
- Feeling of distortion or that you are living in a fantasy, life feels unreal.
- Feeling as if you don't belong, as if you are invisible to others, or as if you are a total stranger.

- A strong feeling that you are lost and don't know who you are. A feeling of being someone other than you thought you were before and wanting to find your "true self."
- Experiencing a loss of ego or personal identities, old belief systems and programs; feeling disassociated or fragmented; Experiencing multidimensional consciousness. Feeling "different" in general.
- Feeling like you are dying

Now that we have covered some of the many unpleasant or strange symptoms of Ascension, let's review some of the many positive symptoms of waking up, raising your vibrational frequency and going through Ascension.

- Developing new abilities or augmentation of old abilities: increased intuition, psychic abilities, telepathy, clairvoyance, clairaudience, clairsentience, channeling, empathic abilities, intuition, ability to see energy, prophesy, and other similar gifts.
- Beginning to hear or see your spirit guides, Ascended masters, angels or E.T.s or feeling their presence.
- Feeling a profound connection to God, source, spirit like you have never had before.
- Sudden interest in space, the stars and extraterrestrials.
- Sudden changes in your life.
- Developing an attraction to specific crystals and stones.
- Sudden urge to learn everything about metaphysics and alchemy.
- Becoming more service-to-others oriented.
- Becoming more heart and love centered.
- Ego begins to fall away or dissolve.

31

- Feeling a need to meditate daily or have a meditation practice.
- Realizing and claiming your sovereignty.
- Developing an ability to see and feel energy. • Feeling happy for the first time in your life
- Sudden need to move to a different place.
- Quitting your job to do something that is more in alignment with your purpose.
- Feeling more connected to nature and animals and appreciating them more.
- Increased sensitivity to all living things including plants, flowers, trees.
- An extreme desire to spend more time out in nature, and when you are in nature finding that you are experiencing more positive energy, peace and healing.
- A strong desire to travel the world and connect with new people, cultures and places.
- Noticing synchronicities daily.
- Noticing number patterns showing up for you daily like 111, 222, 333, 444, 555, 666, 777, 888, 999, 1010, 1111, 1212. You see these numbers everywhere from your email, computer and clocks to signs on the road, driver's licenses and when shopping.
- You think about people you haven't heard from in a long time and then they call you.
- You run into interesting people when you are out and about and they create positive life changing or educational experiences for you or they give you information or messages you need to hear.
- Old low vibrational friends start to disappear out of your life and new higher vibrational friends enter your life.
- Starting to feel intense feelings of love, joy, peace and gratitude like never before.

- You start to love yourself and others unconditionally for first time
- Feeling clarity about your life and situation and where you are going and what you should be doing next.
- Intense feelings of oneness and connectedness with God, all humans and all living creatures.
- Things that you used to worry about or that used to upset you no longer bother you. Instead you feel peace when thinking about them.
- The voice inside your head goes from "monkey brain" and negative thoughts to more space and peace and more positive thoughts.
- You begin noticing pleasant sounds you never paid attention to before, like birds singing or you hear angelic or heavenly choir music.
- You notice which people make you feel happy and energized and which people drain your energy.
- You start making better choices daily.
- Wisdom and amazing information starts pouring from your higher self or spirit into your human brain, and you begin to share this wisdom with others.
- You find your life purpose and start living a more purpose filled life.

Part of the Ascension prophesy and what many of us in the spiritual world know about, is that a great solar flash will be coming to Earth, and it will transform every planet and every living thing in our Universe. This solar flash has been mentioned in almost all ancient religions. It is also known as the Rapture, Soul Harvest, Armageddon, Judgement Day, or Samvartaka Fire.

This event has been preplanned for what seems like an eternity and is predicted to happen within the next nine or ten years of my writing this book. It will happen when a substantial enough proportion of humanity has woken up and chosen the light.

Right now, the awakening is happening at a very fast rate. Some people say this solar flash will come from our own sun and others say it will be a massive burst of cosmic waves that will be transmitted from the Central Sun through the black hole in the center of our galaxy and transmitted through our sun. According to prophesy, it will appear on Earth as milky warm liquid light. Also, it is said that humans who are ready spiritually and energetically will experience near instant evolution and transmutation from two-strand double helix DNA Carbon based Life forms into Crystalline Life Forms having a Light Body with Multiple Additional (up to 12) DNA Strands and shall then "Ascend" to 5th Dimensional Earth in their Physical Bodies.

Some people are afraid of this event, but it has been prophesized to be a peaceful rather than a destructive doomsday event, like fear-based people like to tout. In order to make it through this event you need to be mostly love based, to not harbor feelings of ill will against anyone, to be mostly service to others, to be truthful and accountable for all your actions and to focus on positive thoughts, feelings and actions. According to prophesy those who are dark souls and of service to self will not survive the flash and their souls will be taken away for punishment, rehabilitation and learning how to live in balance.

I asked Yeshua if this information is true and he told me that *"yes, this is true"*. He also told me that all human souls stuck on Earth in what we call a ghost form, as well as all demons, will be removed from the planet. The human souls will go directly to heaven and the demons will go somewhere else. He explained to me that the only reason souls have been trapped here without a body in the first place, was because of dark magic from the dark cabal, combined with fear-based teachings that have trapped people for thousands of years so they did not know how to find their way to the light.

Just in case you are having issue believing this, in April and May of 2019 astronomers spotted something they call "unprecedented" while observing the black hole that is closest to our Earth. It was an eruption and massive burst of light or infrared radiation. The scientists have no clue what that was and what would have caused it. We in the spiritual community have a good idea of what caused this. This black hole is called Sagittarius A* and is located in the middle of our Milky Way Galaxy, 26,000 light years from our planet. The scientists who found this light in the black hole were using the Keck II Telescope in Hawaii. The scientists said that this light has reached much brighter flux levels than ever before. They called it "very unusual" compared to historical data from telescopes, including the Keck II. This all being said, even science is showing us what is coming soon to our Earth.

There are many other good and bad effects of Ascension that I did not list because it's just too much information. In the meantime, it would be great if you have mostly or all of the good symptoms of Ascension. However, if you *do* experience any of the negative effects of Ascension it is most important that you:

1. Rule out any actual health problems.
2. Be compassionate, loving and good to yourself. You are not broken. You are just a human going through a major life changing experience.
3. Exercise lots of self-care. Eat a healthy diet, get adequate sleep.
4. Remember we are all in the same boat so you have lots of brothers and sisters who can support you. Seek out other awakened people, lightworkers, spiritual teachers and counselors and share your experiences, and ask for support and input.

I provide spiritual guidance to my clients as a guide and teacher to help them through the Ascension process. If you need some help you can schedule a spiritual guidance session with me at:

http://www.spiritualgrowthjourneys.com

Chapter 2

Who and what are you?

The majority of people on this planet are confused as to who, or what, they really are.

There are a few reasons for this phenomenon. The first reason is that we as a collective of souls chose to come to this classroom with the knowledge of who we are, and our past soul experiences shut down or erased. Some people refer to that as a veil. Of course, this is a temporary shut down and erasure of memories, since you will get them back again when you leave your body.

The other reason people are so confused is due to the dark entities and negative E.T.s who have controlled and enslaved humanity by separating humans from God and from each other with their system of duality. They have done this by teaching us duality in churches, temples, and mosques, in the school system and in society. They have taught humans for thousands of years that we are limited and have no power. However, that has all been a big lie.

The truth is that you are a limitless spirit being and you have the ability to co-create and manifest your dreams with God. Since you were born, people have undoubtedly been telling you that you are limited in different ways, and yet you are not. The dark entities and negative E.T.s on this planet have also used race and religion to keep all human beings separated and at odds with each other. They have deliberately created situations where people turn against each other to protest and riot over issues like race, religion or political party. They have instigated people to commit hate crimes against others by keeping most of us stuck in patterns of separation, fear, ignorance and hate.

In recent times they have used the media to continue this big illusion that we are separated from God and from each other. Of course, this is all far from the real truth. We are all one "human race" and we are connected to each other through the energy of the quantum field, as well as through our Creator as the children of God. Keep in mind that there are some people on Earth, like myself, who were born with psychic abilities or who at some point in their life develop the ability to know the truth about who they really are and so do not experience any duality or separation. We see all humans as our sisters and brothers.

If I ask a person who has their memory erased, "*Who or what are you?*", their answer will almost certainly be their color, religion, race, socio-economic status, hobby or occupation. But these answers are not the truth of who you are. You are not your skin color. You are not your race or religion and you are not your occupation or your social scale. The simplest description of your true identity is that you are a "divine spirit having a human experience". You are the driver in a specific vehicle you have chosen in this lifetime for your journey. You will have many different vehicles during your soul journey. According to the laws of Quantum Physics and Spiritual Dynamics, you are made of energy, frequency and vibration just like everything else that exists in this universe and throughout all time, space and dimensions. You come from God and you will return to God. You are *in* the world, but you are not *of* the world.

What that means, is that the "you" occupying a human body on Earth right now, existed in other dimensions and possibly other worlds before you came to this planet. Most of us who are here now are very old souls. When I say old, I am talking hundreds of thousands or maybe billions of years old. Think of your physical body as a sort of puppet and your soul is the puppeteer. Imagine in your mind that if God was a big block of ice water and you took millions of small chips out of that ice, the chips you remove are still ice water — they may *look* different and have different shapes and sizes but they are still ice water. So too are you related to your source God creator. Each and every planet, person and living thing is a unique expression of God. The simplest description of who and what you are is that "you are love" because you were created out of love by an unconditionally loving creator.

The more complex version of what and who you are, is that you are a divine spirit being (also known as a soul) who has a physical body, etheric body, energy body, astral body, mental body, and emotional body. You also have something known as your higher self and over soul that calls the shots. Your energy body is made up of 12 chakras, seven of which are considered "major" chakras (energy centers).

There are many people who have religious doctrine belief systems of duality, who are convinced that you cannot be a "divine" spirit. This is actually a false belief since we all come from divine source creator God, and that God is part of us since we are the smaller chips of the ice block, thus our spirit in its purest form is divine. Also, in the Bible Yeshua said, *"You will do greater things than I"*. If that is true, then we are divine because he was a divine spirit who stated that we are greater than him. This divinity has nothing to do with being an *actual* God. We are not Gods, but we are *part* of God and we were birthed from the womb of God.

Now, let us discuss the various aspects of what makes up "you". I will to be presenting you with very brief descriptions of each of these, because each aspect of you alone can make up an entire book of information. If you wish to learn more about each of the aspects of yourself, I highly recommend researching each part on your own.

1. **Your physical body:** You already know that you are made of flesh and blood and bone, but did you know that your body is like an entire universe filled with billions of inhabitants? Every single cell, bacteria and mitochondria in your body is alive and make up entire cities in the universe that is you. You even have tiny little microscopic bugs living on your eyelashes and

eyebrows! Every cell that makes up your physical body is a vibrating mass of Consciousness in formation. This accounts for why you can talk to your body and create healing. Your body has its own intelligence. Your heart even has a brain.

According to Heart Math, LLC, *"the human heart, in addition to its other functions, possesses a heart-brain composed of about 40,000 neurons that can sense, feel, learn and remember. The heart brain sends messages to the head brain about how the body feels and more. The heart's complex intrinsic nervous system, the heart brain, is an intricate network of several types of neurons, neurotransmitters, proteins and support cells, like those found in the brain proper. Research has shown that the heart communicates to the brain in several major ways and acts independently of the cranial brain."*

2. **Your mental body:** There is so much involved with the mental body that it could fill an entire book, by itself.

   My simplified version is that your mental body is attached to your brain and attached to your crown chakra. Your mental body consists of subconscious and conscious thoughts, perceptions, beliefs, intelligence, memories, ideas, education, information and more, all of which are stored within your human brain and also comprise your mental body. All of these things that you store within your mental body carry an energy, a frequency and a vibration.

   Your conscious thoughts are the ones that you know about and can speak, write, repeat and remember. Your subconscious thoughts, perceptions and beliefs are those that stay in the back of your mind and play over and over like a recording running in the background, however you are not aware that they are there and you can only access them through special modalities like meditation, healing and hypnosis. These subconscious thoughts, perceptions and beliefs are created by everything that you have seen and heard from your family, friends, neighbors, teachers, society, media, TV, movies, books, etc. since you were in your mother's womb and able to hear.

You also get subconscious thoughts through past lifetime trauma and memories along with inherited information through your DNA. However, the main difference is that you cannot *remember* your subconscious thoughts, perceptions and beliefs, yet they are in the background running a program that impacts your life 24/7. Your subconscious mind that is part of your mental body that is basically like a giant computer program that runs your life. According to scientists like Bruce H. Lipton, PhD, 95% of your life is operated by a subconscious mind program that comes from other people. Most of these programs are negative, damaging and destructive to your life.

The good news is that you can change the negative programs running your life through practices such as constant repetition of mantras, forming new habits, hypnotherapy, emotional code modalities, healing modalities and energy psychology. There are other ways to reprogram and heal your subconscious mind, but the important thing is that you take action as soon as possible, because if 95% of your life is run by negative subconscious programming that is immensely important and has a huge impact on your Ascension.

3. **Your emotional body:** The emotional body is where you experience and store all your emotions, feelings, passions and desires. The emotional body is more subtle than the energy body, which I will cover later.

When you use your emotional body, you are able to experience intense emotions, including both lower and higher emotions ranging from anger, fear, stress and irritation to love, compassion, happiness and many more. The emotional body has a 100% impact on all your other bodies, especially your physical body.

Bruce H. Lipton and other scientists have found that negative conscious and subconscious emotions or emotional stress cause 98% of all health problems in the body and the other 2% are caused by inherited emotional stress. Basically, negative emotions when not experienced and promptly healed or dealt with properly will harm you on many levels, especially the physical. Negative emotions are very low vibration and they lower *your* vibration, and if they are not dealt with can prevent your Ascension process. Positive emotions have a high vibration and raise your vibration, assisting you with your Ascension process.

It is very important that you — as a human being with a human brain and body — always allow yourself to experience and feel both negative and positive emotions, and then work on processing, clearing and healing the negative emotions immediately. On the contrary, positive emotions like joy, happiness and love create healing on all levels of all your bodies, and also raise your vibrations. Therefore, it is very important to focus on and create as many positive emotions and emotional experiences as possible.

4. **Your soul/spirit:** The most important thing to remember is that your soul was created a very long time ago by God and it has no end. Your soul can never be destroyed, and it holds all the memories of all the lifetimes you have lived in various bodies on Earth, on other planets and in other dimensions.

According to Quantum Physics, matter or energy cannot be destroyed and you are energy. The divine spirit that lives within your physical body goes on forever. Eventually all souls rejoin with the creator source who made them, but until that time your soul is on a journey of constant learning, experiencing, and growing closer in your relationship with your creator. When all souls were originally created at their beginning, they all started out at the same level or dimension. As souls go through their evolution or journey, they move up a ladder of sorts to reach higher dimensions and consciousness levels.

A good example would be that angels exist at a very high dimensional level. A human soul or E.T. soul could eventually reach a level where they could become an angel in a higher dimension. However, once you reach that level you cannot go backwards. Your soul can only move in one direction. Your soul keeps getting promotions, but you cannot get a demotion.

Your soul also belongs to a soul group or soul family. Sometimes you come back to Earth or other planets with the same soul group or family. Each time you return you are like members of an acting troupe, with each one of you playing a different role each time. Sometimes you may be the mother and other times you may be the sister or a scorned lover. I will discuss reincarnation later in the book.

All souls that spring forth and are birthed from source are unique expressions of source but are created for different positions and different dimensions. As souls progress through their journey and move up the dimensional ladder to higher dimensions, some souls will eventually become an angelic being or angel in a very high dimension. Not all souls will become angels; however, it is possible for angels to incarnate into human bodies. An angel incarnating into 3D Earth has to lower their density to be here, but as soon as they leave this place they are back to where they were before they left, because it is a temporary damper.

There are some souls living on Earth that were just created to be in human bodies, some souls were created to be in E.T. bodies before they became humans, and there are also angelic beings currently in human bodies who are here for the Great Awakening and creation of New Earth. When you are in soul or spirit form without your body, you are freed from the constraints of time and space; you are indestructible and free from aging, starvation, and exposure to the elements. Many people who have had Near Death Experiences, have shared that most people's souls, when they are in heaven, look like they did in their early 30s.

Something fascinating that really blew my mind while I was channeling this information from Yeshua, is that Satan has a soul and he is a dark or what people call "evil" and very ancient extraterrestrial. The demons on Earth right now were created by Satan and they do not have souls. They are interdimensional beings and similar to an artificial intelligence that is completely controlled by Satan. They have absolutely no free will. They purely do the bidding of Satan. Demons can go inside humans and possess them.

As a divine spirit and child of God you have been given free will to make choices between good and bad, and how you will learn on your journey. You also are a sovereign spirit. What that means is that you rule over you and God rules over you. You have complete control over yourself. But no other being has the right to control you or your journey. Unfortunately, as the planet has been in lockdown for thousands of years, our sovereignty while on Earth has been taken away by the dark entities controlling our planet.

Since our Earth was freed by benevolent extraterrestrials in 2019, we now have our sovereignty back; however, everyone needs to wake up and *claim* that sovereignty. Most humans are living as though they do not have any free will or sovereignty. This is already changing, as people are waking up to their own divinity.

5. **Your etheric body:** The etheric body or ether-body is the subtle body that is the lowest layer of the human energy field or aura. It is in immediate contact with the human physical body and helps sustain the physical body and connect it with the higher bodies. All your emotions show up in your etheric body first, before impacting your physical body in either a negative or positive way. Then those emotions continue into your energy body.

6. **Your Energy body:** Some people, including myself, are able to see peoples' energy bodies. Some of us perceive it as a white energy layer that protrudes from and lays around the outside of the physical body. Some people also see the colors of the energy body. You may have heard the term "aura", which is basically another name for what your energy body looks like to those who can see it. Some also call it your "auric field".

The reason you may see colors around people is that your energy body or "aura" is made of 12 chakras with seven of those being the "major" chakras that effect your physical body. Each chakra has a specific color of the rainbow.

In 1939 a Russian scientist named Semyon Kirlian invented a form of photography that enabled him to take photos of people's auras. Over the years, aura photography — also known as Kirlian photography — has been improved greatly, to where you can now have a full consultation with someone who specializes in this field and owns the aura photography equipment. Even though each chakra has a specific color, your auric field can show different chakra colors around you, based on what is going on in your life or with your emotional body and emotions.

For example, someone who has a lot of violet colors is very spiritual. Someone with a lot of green is a healer or has healing abilities. If you want to learn more about energy chakras, what they are, how to clear, protect, heal and balance the chakras, I offer classes and private sessions on Chakra balancing for people located anywhere in the world.

You can also do some research into the chakra system on your own. Each of the seven major chakras has an impact on your physical body. If any of your chakras are out of balance or blocked, it can cause health problems in your physical body. Illness always shows up in the chakras first before going into the physical manifestation. When your chakras are healthy, they spin clockwise at a specific vibration. In this book I am briefly covering the seven major chakras because they are the ones that I feel are most important because they all directly impact your physical body. The seven major chakras are:

1st Chakra – Root Chakra - located where your tail bone is and is the color red 2nd Chakra – Sacral – located between your tailbone and belly button and is the color orange.

3rd Chakra – Solar Plexus – located between your belly button and rib cage and is the color yellow like the sun

4th Chakra – Heart center – located where your heart is and is the color green 5th Chakra – Throat and is located at the base of your throat and is the color turquoise blue or light blue

6th Chakra – 3rd Eye – located over your pineal gland between your eyes and is the color indigo blue

7th Chakra – Crown – located on top of head and is the color white and connects you with your higher self and God Source.

This chart below shows the chakra colors and locations on the body.

7. **<u>Your light body or astral body:</u>** The astral body, which is sometimes called the light body, is basically the vehicle that carries the soul from your physical body into the higher dimensions. Your soul maintains

47

your astral body. The astral body is what we use when we have out-of-body experiences and astral project ourselves to different places. Astral travel or astral projection is the process by which a part of your soul leaves the body to travel through the astral plane. The astral plane is a matrix of electromagnetic ley lines that interconnect throughout the universe to create a magnetic field of travel. Our bodies have an electromagnetic field and use it to sustain ourselves, so it is easy for the soul to
use this electromagnetic field to travel on the electromagnetic ley lines of space, time and dimensions.

The process of Astral Travel is a very complicated subject and one that I assist my clients with, in private sessions.

Have you ever done astral projection? If you have experienced it, then you may have seen a silver cord. Some people refer to the silver cord a your "life thread" because it supplies energy to your physical body and also because if it were to be cut away, your physical body would die. Your silver cord or life cord connects your soul to your body and through your central nervous system. Many people who have been put under hypnosis or had near-death experiences have seen their silver cord, as have people who astral travel during sleep or meditation. The silver cord has been mentioned in many ancient religions, including Tibetan Buddhism, Ancient Egyptian Mystery School teachings, Hinduism and Judaism. The Holy Bible also mentions your silver cord.

"Or ever the silver cord be loosed...Then shall the dust return to the earth as it was: and the spirit shall return unto God who gave it (Ecclesiastes 12:6-7)"

If you want to travel out of your body either at night or during meditation, it is dangerous because your physical body is left alone and open to any demonic entities that wish to take you over. If you are going to engage in this type of risky activity, I highly recommend you use some hematite and similar grounding crystals while you are astral projecting or traveling, as well as black tourmaline and selenite to keep away dark entities. Also, I recommend you ask out loud for your angels, Archangel Michael and God to protect you while you are traveling. Otherwise, you can be safer by fractalization of your soul like the horcruxes in Harry Potter. You can splinter out a piece of your astral body or consciousness that can go out into the astral realms, different time periods, different dimensions, and different planets.

Many people do this regularly during dream time and have no clue they are doing it. They just think they were dreaming. Some people even go back and forth over to what we call "heaven" while they are sleeping.

When I first began to astral travel, before I learned how to do it properly, I would leave Earth and go far out into space and wind up in the black void looking down at our universe. This was terrifying and I would freak out and come flying back into my body at the speed of light, slamming into my body so hard that my body would jump a foot or two. It was a very frightening experience!

If you are not already an expert, I would highly recommend working with one before you try it out yourself, primarily to avoid bad experiences. Another danger with astral travel is that there are dark entities that could attach to you and you could bring them back home. Again, make sure you protect yourself with prayer and ask your angels out loud to protect you, when you astral travel or do astral projection.

8. **<u>Your higher self:</u>** Your higher self is basically the person you want to evolve into and *will* evolve into when you become enlightened. It's the best version of you; the version that knows your past, present and future and everything about you.

    Your higher self is both separate from and a part of you. Your higher self is the best version of you and is separate from your ego. Your higher self does not have the basic human instincts and desires that your human brain has. It transcends those. It is always pure, confident, connected to source at all times and is at peace. It doesn't feel fear or suffering, instead it expresses unconditional love. Your past life memories are stored with your higher self as well as your soul and oversoul.

    When you hear people say, "*you need to connect with your higher self*", or "*ask you higher self*", this is what we are speaking of. Many people have lost their connection to their higher self, and as a result they expect to get all the answers for their life, spirituality and other areas from other people. Sadly, this is how phony gurus have been able to control many people. When people are searching for answers outside of themselves, they run to all sorts of "gurus" for the spiritual answers.

    You never need to run to anyone for the answers to your personal spiritual questions, once you learn how to connect with your higher self, God, your spirit guides and angels. Many people feel compelled to always get approval from others. When you learn to connect with your higher self and go within yourself, you learn that you only need approval from yourself and God. Your higher self holds you accountable for all your thoughts, speech and actions at all times. You cannot pull anything over on your higher self because it sees all and knows all. When you master connecting to your higher self, which is something I teach my clients, then you have access to an unlimited library of answers.

9. **Your oversoul:** Definition of oversoul from Merriam-Webster dictionary: "*The absolute reality and basis of all existences conceived as a spiritual being in which the ideal nature imperfectly manifested in human beings is perfectly realized.*"

   Some humans' souls have an oversoul. All the memories of every lifetime you have lived resides with your soul and also with your oversoul. The oversoul works a bit like a parent of several souls. It is constantly monitoring all its under-souls at the same time. These souls all co-exist at the same time in a way similar to the strings on a guitar. There are many strings on the guitar but the guitar itself holds the strings together and each string plays a different note. Each soul that is part of an oversoul has a job or role they are playing, either in higher dimensions or on Earth in a body. If you want to learn more about the oversoul, please research it on your own because it is a topic so complex that it would fill a book.

Your body, mind and spirit, along with all the parts that make up "you", all have a direct impact and effect on each other. When you ignore your physical body and fail to take care of it, you develop health problems that can lead to a spiritual disconnect from creator source. The reason is that you were gifted with this body that is the temple of the Holy Spirit. When you fail to take care of yourself, it is like a slap in the face to God source who gave you this beautiful gift of this life in a human body.

I will be talking more about your health later in this book. When you have a spiritual disconnect from God or from all of humanity or the unity consciousness you can also develop physical, emotional, and spiritual problems and illnesses. It is important that your consciousness and higher self be fully connected and tuned into your physical body at all times. People who have a disconnect between their body, mind and spirit sometimes discover that they have had a serious health issue brewing inside of them for a while but because they were not tuned in, they had no clue. It is imperative to always be tuned in to your body, so that when something goes wrong with your health, you are able to catch it at the beginning when it can be readily treated and healed.

Chapter 3

Who and What Is God?

Everyone calls God by a different name, based on their religious or spiritual training and belief system. Everyone also has their own idea of what God looks like, where God is from and who God *is* based on their upbringing, culture, beliefs, life experience and other variables.

Throughout history, ancient religions worshipped both female Goddesses and male Gods of all types. No matter what your beliefs or religion, the truth is that there is only one Divine Source Creator from whom everything sprung forth over all time, space and dimensions. This is the one true God who made your soul.

In Christianity and Judaism, they have created an image of God in which God is a man (heavenly father) with a beard who sits on a throne in a place called Heaven which is located up in the sky somewhere, and He created us in his image.

This information is not true. How do I know? I have had a few near-death experiences and I am a channel and clairvoyant, so I receive my answers directly from source. The major patriarchal religions have also taught humans that God always judges you and will punish you. Their God is one who is jealous and angry and destroys armies and entire cities, asks you to sacrifice your child on an altar and even kills your baby.

This image and belief in God has been spread by the dark forces who run the planet, and was created to keep you trapped in a place of fear. These same religions have taught you that you are separate from God and need a male priest, rabbi, Imam or pastor to intercede on your behalf with God. This entire system of duality and separation from God was purposefully orchestrated for thousands of years by the very dark beings who have been running the show on Earth up until the present day.

My own parents raised me with the belief that God was always watching me, judging me and would punish me if I did anything wrong. Most of my life — until I started to channel, get downloads and hear God speak directly to me — I was terrified. Many other people on Earth are also afraid of God because they are stuck in a duality, fear-based religion. These major religions and the information they teach were all created to control humans, to create wars over religion, to create mass suffering and to take people's money and land. They have convinced everyone that we are totally separate from God and that we are "not worthy". Now we are finally all waking up as a collective and seeing the truth for the first time in thousands of years.

Now that I told you who and what God is "*not*", I will tell you more about who and what God really *is*.
The most important thing to know is that God is not a man who made us in his image. God is the energy, frequency and vibration of unconditional love. God has both masculine and feminine energies and is ageless and timeless just like your own divine spirit. God is not a person or being sitting on a throne somewhere. God simply *is*. In the Bible, when Moses asked God who he was, God replied "*I am that I am*". God is the creator of everything that was and is and is to come in all time, space, places and dimensions. God keeps creating and that creation process goes on forever and has no time and no end. The location of God is all around you and inside of you. You are part of God and God made you.

God also made endless numbers of planets and different types of life and beings on all those planets. We cannot be made in the image of God because there are beings on other planets that look like giant insects or little grey guys with big heads and bug eyes. That is because everything that God makes is all a unique expression of the creation process.

Humans may have been created in the image of Gods but those Gods were an advanced race of Extraterrestrial beings who altered our DNA. Many of the female and male Gods you see in all ancient religions were merely Extraterrestrials who came to Earth and had advanced devices, ships, weapons, clothing and tools. They might have also had special abilities, like levitation, that humans did not have. The humans back then believed they were Gods and built statues, created art and carved stories about them in stone to remember them. If you have ever watched the show Ancient Aliens or any TV shows about archaeology, then you understand what I am writing about.

As I mentioned earlier, the God of the Jewish and Christian Bible is a wrathful vengeful God who wipes out Earth with floods, plagues, famines, destroying armies, cities and even people along with asking you to sacrifice your only child. The true God, which is the Divine Mother Father Source Creator of Unconditional love, would never harm any of its creation. That God loves you unconditionally, wants you to be happy and healthy and wants to have a close relationship with you. God never judges you. God's main job is being the frequency of love and creation.

When you die, you are given a life review and as it says in the Holy Bible, "You are judged by the deeds that you do on Earth". However, the judge is not God. We are all given a life review where we are shown our entire life, both the good and the bad. We are held accountable for any bad things we have done while on Earth or on other planets or in other dimensions. If you participated in things on Earth that are minor sins like cheating on a spouse or girlfriend, swearing at your family, being rude or disrespectful, or similar low level sins, then you will be held accountable by your spirit guides and guardian angels and they will assist you to make amends for what you did. These are all part of your learning experiences and soul journey.

How you make amends for bad behavior will be decided between you and your team on the other side. However, when someone purposefully commits a serious crime, without any remorse, on Earth or on other planets where they ruin one or more lives, or kill one or more humans, that soul who committed the atrocities will be judged by a tribunal of the highest dimension celestial and angelic beings.

Up until 2012 the world was in a lockdown matrix that included Karma and what is called the "Wheel of Samsara". In Buddhism, this means that you are stuck in an endless cycle of repeated birth, mundane existence and dying again. Your lifetimes are filled with suffering and difficulty based on your ignorance and bad things you did in previous lifetimes.

Many people were tricked by false light beings into signing life contracts that included extensive suffering. This Karma was never created by our source creator God. It was created by the dark forces that have been ruling over Earth. In 2012 the Lords of Karma were shut down and Karma was removed from our planet. Humans no longer have karmic contracts. Now we instead have the punishment I just discussed which is for beings who commit serious crimes and then we have what I call the "Universe Boomerang", which is comprised of all the energy and vibration that makes up us and the universe.

Basically, everything you do, think, feel or say has either a good or bad energy vibration. That vibration goes into the universal energy field whenever you do something, say something or think something and it comes right back to you. Because of the Ascension our planet is going through right now, we are all able to instantly manifest based on our thoughts, feelings, words and actions. If you are thinking or doing bad things, it will come back to you in the form of negative things happening to your body or your life. If you do positive things and think positive thoughts, you will get back positive energy. In the Bible there is a story about Jesus cursing a fig tree and it shrivels up and dies. He may not have actually done that, but it's a parable to teach you that your words are spells and your words have power to manifest. Be mindful of all your thoughts, words, and actions.

If you are trying to seek God and want to know where God lives, all you have to do is look around you and also look within. The major religions taught false beliefs that God lives up in the sky in this heaven place, but that story is not true. God is definitely in heaven, but heaven is not located up in the sky. God is everywhere. God is around you and all over the Earth. God is located in the earth and in every planet and every living thing ever created. God is in every rock, every grain of sand, every drop of water and God is inside you since you are a divine expression and creation of God.

When you are in heaven you are always and forever basking in the loving presence of God. In heaven, you are closer to God than you will ever be when you are in a body. If you are wondering where heaven is located, it is actually in another dimension. When you go there after you die, you will either walk through a door of light, a portal, or a tunnel. It depends on your situation. Millions of people have had near-death experiences and the ones who have shared the experience, including myself, all say that the way you pass over to heaven is different for each of us — but it usually involves a door, a portal or a tunnel.

There are many different levels and dimensions of what people call Heaven, it is not all located in a single dimension. Gaia or Mother Earth is our temporary home and a big classroom. What we call Heaven, is our real home. All our friends and family from this lifetime and past lifetimes are there, unless they have incarnated back into a body for more learning experiences on their journey.

I am not going to go into great detail about heaven in this book because there would be too much information and there are already many fantastic books written on the subject by people who have had near-death experiences or are psychic mediums. In addition, interpretations of heaven can be different because how one experiences heaven can be unique to each person.

Here are a few things I *will* point out about heaven, based on my own near-death experiences, along with channeled messages and downloads I have received from God source and Yeshua.

First of all, the colors in heaven are so incredible that there are no colors like them on Earth. When you are in heaven there is no time like we know it on Earth. The past, present and future all happen at same time. Time is like a big circle that goes round and round without end on the other side. When you are in heaven there are beings there from other planets and dimensions, not just humans. There are also angels in heaven and very high dimensional celestial beings. When you are in heaven the feeling you get is one of 100% unconditional love because there you are basking in the unconditional love of God forever.

You are able to look at your akashic records to review all your past soul experiences throughout time, space and dimensions. There are no organized religions in heaven because there is only the single religion of love and peace. There are buildings you can go to that are similar to churches, where you can gather with others and pray and experience similar to what you had on Earth, but there are multiple types of religions and denominations. You do not have to eat or sleep when you are in heaven because you don't have a body you must sustain with energy, however if you want to eat or sleep because it's something you enjoy, then you can.

If you want to know more about heaven, a good book to read is "*The After Life Interviews*" by Jeffrey A. Marks. There are 2 volumes. Jeffrey is a psychic medium who sat with people whose loved ones passed and he interviewed 100s of souls on the other side. He asked them all the major questions concerning death, heaven, religion, and other topics that most of us humans have.

The opposite of heaven is hell. Hell is real but it's not a specific place that has fire and brimstone, where Satan sits on a throne. There are places like that below the Earth and on other planets, but those places are not the one location known as hell. Sometimes the Earth might seem like hell, but fortunately we are about to turn it into a heaven.

Hell is actually a state of consciousness, where beings and souls who have turned away from God exist. Hell is a dark state of consciousness that is devoid of the light of God. When someone is in hell they can see all the things happening both in heaven and on planet Earth (or whatever planet they are from), but they are in a cellular prison of sorts where they cannot engage with anyone in those places. They are also completely isolated from other souls and beings.

The beings and souls who go to a hell state when they leave their body, are ones who have made a conscious free will choice to turn their backs on the light of God, on love and on all that is good. These beings or souls who get put into a hell isolation are people like Hitler, Stalin, murderers, rapists, pedophiles, drug dealers, sex traffickers, terrorists, abusers, people who torture and kill pets and other animals, along with a host of horrible evil beings. They have souls that are very dark.

Every soul comes from God, including the dark ones who turn away from the light. Every soul on Earth has free will and is able to choose between good and evil, light and dark. There are many spiritual people teaching that there is no good or bad and everything "just is." That is false information because we have free will and personal accountability. It is not okay for someone to go murder a child. We cannot simply turn our back and say "it just is" and there is no "good or bad". If we walk around accepting bad people and allowing them to do bad things, the world would be destroyed by evil. We have to hold all people accountable for their actions.

There are two types of people, fear-based people and love-based people. If you are a mostly love-based person, then you will definitely be going to heaven. Churches and religions may have taught you that unless you are perfect all the time — or unless you worship Jesus — that you are not going to heaven. This is a lie. Everyone who is a primarily good person eventually goes to the same heavenly dimension, no matter what religion or lack of religion they had in their life. Remember that in the Holy Bible, Romans 2:6, it said *you will be judged by the deeds you do*. If you do good things you have nothing to worry about, as to where you will go when you leave your body. However, if you are a fear-based, mean, nasty, evil, or dark soul, then you could end up in the dark isolation booth located in another dimension. It is up to you since you have free will to choose the light or the darkness. Every soul, both good and bad, comes from God. Eventually the dark souls get rehabilitated and will be afforded another chance. First, they are held accountable and face whatever punishment the heavenly tribunal decides to give them.

Now that we talked about heaven and hell, I would like to talk about the opposite of Creator God, which is Lucifer and Satan. Many people think they are the same person, but Lucifer and Satan are two different beings. Lucifer was a fallen angel who turned against God; he has been in exile for a very long time. Lucifer left Satan in charge of Earth. Satan is not an angel, he is a very old advanced extraterrestrial. The kind of powerful extraterrestrial that people worshipped as a God in ancient times on Earth. Satan and Lucifer both have souls and both have free will, but they choose to turn away from God and destroy humanity by causing wars, famine, starvation, illness, suffering and pain. Satan and his minions suck energy from suffering humans. Their favorite form of food is your fear, pain and suffering. The more you stay in a place of fear, pain or suffering the more they gain.

Satan has billions of minions working for him that we call demons. Demons do not have souls and they do not have free will. They were created by Satan to do his bidding and work to destroy our Mother Gaia (Earth) and all the living things on her. Demons are a form of artificial intelligence. Because they do not have free will or a soul they do not have any compassion or love, and they cannot be negotiated with. If you have a demon in your home or you have a demonic attachment, you cannot negotiate with it. Instead you need to call in angels or work with shaman, lightworkers or demonologists to get rid of the demon or destroy it.

Another thing to discuss is the concept of multi dimensions.

God exists in all time, space and dimensions. There are over 22 different dimensions starting with first dimension. Earth is currently in the third dimension but we are heading for the fifth dimension. You are a multi-dimensional being and just like God is in all dimensions at all times, your soul is able to travel to and through different dimensions.

Celestial beings and angels reside in the highest dimensions, but there are many different types of beings living in each and every dimension. Many people, like myself, travel into other dimensions either through meditation or while they sleep. Some people remember their interdimensional journeys and some people don't. There are also elemental beings here on Earth and on other planets who do not live in our dimension but are able to pop in and out of our dimension whenever they want.

Some of these include faeries, gnomes, elves, leprechauns, unicorns, banshees, djinn, pegasus, water guardians, forest guardians, centaurs, yeti, bigfoot and many others. I have known many very brilliant and sane people who have had experiences seeing these beings. Hundreds of thousands of people worldwide have experienced seeing them. Many stories you hear that you might think are just made up, are actually based on truth about actual beings that some people who are tuned into their third eye have seen. I have known people who were elemental beings in past lifetimes.

I am going to end this chapter by discussing someone who is sometimes referred to as God, but you know him as Jesus Christ. Christian religion has taught people that Jesus was God and the son of God, but if you read the Bible word for word and study archaeology and history you will learn that he told everyone that he was *not* God and that we are *all* children of God. He also told us that we would do greater things than he did.

People in the spiritual community along with all lightworkers and starseeds are well aware that Jesus was not God, but instead he was an ascended master and the boss of what we call Christ Consciousness.

For those of you who do not know about Christ Consciousness, it is a group of very high dimensional, Christed and high vibrational loving compassionate beings who are ascended masters. These beings have all attained enlightenment and have been on Earth before as spiritual teachers, healers and wayshowers. Many of these beings also had some supernatural powers that made them seem like a God. Some of the members of Christ Consciousness include Yeshua, Buddha, Sananda, Matreya, Mother Mary, Mary Magdalene, White Buffalo Calf Woman and many others.

Yeshua (Jesus) is also *my* boss, because I am here working for him and continuing his teachings. When the Christ was born, the name he was given by his parents in Aramaic and Hebrew was Yeshua Ben Joseph. Historically, he was also called Yeshua Ben Pantera. When I ask him for help, I always refer to him as Yeshua.

One important reason to refer to him by his real name is that when you look at gematria, which is an ancient number system used by the dark cabal, astrologers and ancient mystics, his name was translated by the cabal into Latin and changed to Jesu. Then it was changed in King James Bible into the name Jesus. When his Hebrew Name was changed into Latin, they gave him the name Jesu which has the same gematria as Satan, number 330 in English and 55 in simple Gematria. The name that King James gave him was Jesus in English, which is same Gematria as Lucifer, number 444. The reason they did this, was to trick you into praying to Lucifer and Satan.

When you pray or talk to him, you can call him whatever you want, because I believe your personal intention creates an energy, frequency, and vibration. However, he told me that he will answer to people praying in the name of Jesus and who have good intention, however, he prefers his real name of Yeshua. So, when I talk with him or pray to him, that is the name I use.

Over the years he has told me many truths about his lifetime that are not in the Holy Bible, including things like where he lived, where and what he studied and why he died the way he did. I am very grateful to have developed the ability to hear him speak to me after my children were born. However, I am not special because you too can learn how to speak with him, with God and with other beings, so that you are able to receive the truth direct from source and be your own guru.

In chapter 11, I will be covering how to communicate with and hear God, Jesus and other beings. Because this book is a 101 or beginning level book, I have gone over only some basics about God, Heaven, and a few other topics associated with God. To learn more, you can work with me in private session or do your own research. There are thousands of books, websites and information pieces out in the world. You need to find your own truth, just like I have my own truth.

Chapter 4

Reincarnation and the Lie Called Karma

Definition of Karma from the Merriam Webster Dictionary:

"Karma is the force generated by a person's actions held in Hinduism and Buddhism to perpetuate transmigration and in its ethical consequences to determine the nature of the person's next existence; broadly: such a force considered as affecting the events of one's life."

The concept of Karma has been around for thousands of years. This concept came primarily from the Buddhist and Hindu religions as well as certain other religions. Many people have lots of questions about Karma, the laws of Karma, the Karma they have generated and the connection between God and Karma.

First of all, God does not have anything to do with Karma since God does not judge. Unfortunately, Karma has been a big lie created by the dark cabal thousands of years ago in order to keep humanity trapped in what is called the Wheel of Samsara. We became stuck in a matrix that was rigged in such a way that we all believed that whatever we did would create this Karma and force us to come back over and over again to experience pain and suffering for the purpose of this Karma we created.

Many of us have been tricked into suffering contracts by false light beings (dark and evil beings disguised as good). Also, the dark souls and evil entities who hide inside human bodies on Earth have been circulating in and out of a revolving door for thousands of years. They die and then come back immediately in another body to cause more evil, chaos and destruction on the planet. Some of these evil beings who come back over and over again, include people like Hitler, Stalin and serial killers. Somehow the evil beings seem to have been exempt from the Karma trap system they established on Earth.

Karma is a super complicated subject and since I am not an expert on Karma, I am just touching upon a little information about it here. What I would like for you all to know, is that as of 2012 the Lords of Karma have been shut down and Karma is not actually a thing anymore. If you were born before 2012 any Karma contracts you signed are now null and void. The children coming in after 2012 do not *have* Karma.

Now there are only two important concepts you need to know and understand. First, if you do very bad things on Earth, you will be held accountable, then you will receive some sort of punishment and you will receive a soul rehabilitation that could take hundreds, thousands, millions or even *billions* of years.

Second, the universe is a boomerang. What you put into the energy field you will receive back immediately. We are now manifesting instantly, due to the huge energy and DNA changes on Earth as we head towards 5D. Everything you think, say, or do will go into the universal energy and come back to you somehow. In most cases this will happen while you are still alive in this body, no reincarnation to fulfill Karma necessary.

Another subject related to Karma is "Reincarnation".

If you are wondering how reincarnation relates to Ascension, it is a very simple concept. Basically, each time you reincarnate, you are learning lessons and hopefully improving yourself with each time. If you keep improving, then you are headed in a positive direction for Ascension of your soul and consciousness. If you keep reincarnating but never improving or becoming a more loving, compassionate, and peaceful being, then you have not learned any lessons and you will not be able to Ascend here on Earth. Maybe sometime in the future — on another planet — you will be able to Ascend. This all reminds me of one of the definitions of insanity, which is doing the same thing over and over again, while expecting a different outcome. The dark souls who keep reincarnating are basically insane. They are devoid of love and compassion and each time they reincarnate they repeat the same or similar evil deeds.

The primary reason we keep coming back to Earth is that some of us were stuck in a trap and couldn't leave. Second, we come here to this giant classroom to learn lessons.

Please keep in mind that not everyone reincarnates. Some souls have only been in a body one time and after returning home to what we call "heaven" may not incarnate into a body ever again. I know many people who have come to Earth for the first time in history for the purpose of this Great Awakening and Ascension. They came from other planets, universes, and even other dimensions.

Also, please note that when you reincarnate into a new physical body, it may not even happen on Earth. You could come back on another planet in another star system. The number of times you incarnate into a physical body is up to you, since you have free will to choose. There are some souls like me who have only been on Earth a few times. This is the first time I have been in a physical body on Earth in 2,000 years and before that I was here six other times.

There are many humans on this Earth whose souls are extraterrestrial, celestial or angelic in origin, but there are also souls on Earth who are human souls who have only been in human bodies. Some of us who are here for the Ascension have come from higher dimensions and have had to lower our vibration to match the density of 3D. It is very intense and complicated for us. Many of us struggle with constant physical problems and some souls also struggle with mental problems because it is so hard for us to be in this low density when we come from very high dimensions.

If you are someone who knows that you came from a higher dimension, you need to really good care of yourself, physically, mentally and spiritually beyond what most people normally need to do and you must be super patient, compassionate and loving with yourself at all times.

People like myself, who are not human souls and came here from other places, may spend their entire lives feeling like they never fit in. My mother was one of those people and I, too, feel like I have never fit in. When you are a starseed and you are surrounded by humans who are not starseeds, it makes you feel like you are out of place. I never fit in with the other kids in school because there was something different about me. I was a starseed born with many abilities that human souls usually do not have — intuition, empathy, prophesy, sensing and seeing energy and many more.

People have felt attracted to me since I was young, but they usually are drawn to me to get my advice and help or because they want something from me. I have had very few friends during my lifetime. I never fit into any of the cliques in school, at church or in my neighborhoods I have lived in throughout my life. As a mother I couldn't fit in with the other moms or with the school PTA. When I have been involved in organizations like girl scouts, I was always the outcast. I was even left out when I was in high school choir. A few of the ways to know that you are a starseed from another place, is that you always feel alienated or not part of the group. You feel like you never belong with other people around you or that you even belong on Earth. You may have a constant urge to want to go home, especially since Earth has been such a densely low vibration place.

When you reincarnate, you usually come back with the same soul group of family and friends. Many of us know each other from past lifetimes. It is a bit like being an actor in a

Shakespeare theatre troupe and each time you are here you are playing a different role in a different play.

In some of your lifetimes you may be mother to someone in your group, and then you may come back as the brother of that same person. You can reincarnate into different sexes and you can also reincarnate into animals. Some people who are here now were elementals before they went into a human body. I know several people who were faeries before they reincarnated into a human body now.

The reason those elementals chose to come here *now* and incarnate into a human body is because they are here for the "Big Event", Great Awakening and Ascension of our planet. Back when Karma existed you may have been killed by someone in a past lifetime and come back with that same person again, so they could make it up to you. You have free will, so you decide before you come here, in counsel with your spirit guides and guardian angels, who you will be when you come back and what lessons you are here to learn.

Some people have memories of their past lifetimes and some people even dream about them. People who are psychic or clairvoyant usually have the most information about their past lifetimes. Many of my friends have Starseed children who all remember their past lifetimes, on Earth and on other planets. Many of the millennial children coming in now have most of their past lifetime memories intact and have not come in with the amnesia that others came in with.

When you want to learn about your past lifetimes, there are several things you can do. First, you can pray and ask God and your angels to reveal your past lifetime information to you through your dreams or in meditation. Second, you can develop your third eye or psychic abilities, so you can ask for the answers or remember everything yourself. Finally, you can work with a past life regression hypnotherapist that specializes in helping you uncover your past lifetimes. When we all ascend 100% into 5th dimensional consciousness, we will be able to access our past lifetime memories that have been blocked off from us.

Because of the Wheel of Samsara or Karma trap, many humans have reincarnated to only to lives of pain and suffering. However, some people have chosen pain or suffering in their life plan to either learn lessons or to teach lessons to others.

I will explain this in more detail in the chapter on why you have health problems. The truth is that if there was absolutely no pain or suffering and no evil at all on Earth, then it would not be much of a classroom. You would not leave heaven, and you would not learn much or teach much. I personally have been able to help so many people because of my own pain and suffering and what I learned from those experiences. I love turning lemons into lemonade by using my negative experiences to advise and assist other people.

Another thing that causes much of your pain and suffering in this lifetime or any lifetime — according to the Buddhism — is your Ego. Ego has been necessary for humans to survive in a 3D reality, however when ego is out of balance it can cause pain and suffering to you as well as to other people in your life.

Some people recognize friends and family members from past lifetimes. Not everyone knows who and what they were in those past lifetimes. A lot of people just have a basic feeling that they knew certain people before their current lifetime. A lot of the children coming into the world over the last 20 to 30 years are coming in with full memories of past lifetimes. In my own lifetime I have had the pleasure of connecting with many friends whom I have known before this life. Some of my friends and family were with me in every lifetime and some of them only in one or two. I also know which ones are in my life for the first time.

When you are able to find out what type of relationship you had with current family members in previous lifetimes, it can help you experience some karmic healing. In cases where you hurt family members or friends, or they hurt you, it's good to know this information so that there can be forgiveness and healing. If you do not know if your current friends or family members were with you in past lifetimes or what role you played in previous lives on Earth, there are several ways to find out. You can ask your higher self, guides and angels for the answer, you can go to a psychic medium, you can use tarot cards, you can use meditation for the answers or you can do past life regression with a certified hypnotherapist.

You may discover that some lifetimes were on Earth and others were on other planets. Many people have had lifetimes on other planets. Most the people on Earth right now are old souls who have come here to participate in this big 3D experiment we have been engaged in for thousands of years. The majority of people you know, have lived more than one lifetime here.

If you do not know about this, I highly recommend looking into this information, because it can help you with your Ascension process, especially if you owe someone who is in your life some Karma.

Chapter 5

Your Life Purpose Is Not What You Think

There is a multitude of coaches and spiritual gurus who want to teach you how to figure out your life purpose. Some of these people charge a small fortune for their services. Yeshua told me that the majority of these people teaching about life purpose, are teaching the wrong information. Many of you may have an idea as to what your life purpose is, based on these coaches' and teachers' ideas or opinions, but those ideas may not be right. Yeshua asked me to set the record straight with the truth about what your real-life purpose is. He gave me an entire download about this subject that I will share with you here and now.

Your soul's purpose

Your soul has always had a purpose, ever since you were created and birthed by divine source Mother Father God. Your soul actually has *several* important purposes, and these soul purposes are the same for every soul that has been created.

The number one purpose of your soul is love and happiness.

In fact, His Holiness the Dalai Lama has said, "*I believe that the very purpose of our life is to seek happiness*".

That is the purpose of your soul and it should also flow into your life on Earth in a human body. The reason that your soul purpose is love and happiness is because we were created by an unconditionally loving creator who loves all his/her creation and wants for our happiness.

Our other soul purposes are to constantly learn lessons, raise our vibrational frequency, Ascend, and grow closer to Mother/Father God. After we complete all the lessons and cycles that our soul has chosen to go through, we eventually all have the purpose of returning back to the loving source that created and birthed us. Many of us are striving to reach the level of Christ Consciousness, which is the next level down from Mother Father God but has nothing to do with Christian religion.

There are Ascended Masters known as Christed beings from many religious backgrounds, as well as from other planets and dimensions, who are part of the brother and sisterhood of Christ Consciousness. These Christed beings all came down to Earth to different parts of the world to teach the exact same lessons and concepts like love, kindness, compassion, forgiveness, oneness, unity, divinity, connecting directly with source or God and much more.
There are also scores of Ascended Masters who are not part of Christ Consciousness and they are one level down below Christ Consciousness. Examples of members of Christ Consciousness who came to Earth are Lord Yeshua, Lord Buddha, Blessed Mother Mary, St. Mary Magdalene, White Buffalo Calf Woman, Sananda, Maitreya, Quan Yin, Green Tara, Hathor, and many others. There are also plenty of Christed beings who never came to Earth.

Keep in mind that the lessons you learn are ones that you have chosen to learn because all of us sentient beings have been given free will.

Your life's purpose

Although many people talk about a "*life purpose*", it is really more of a life *mission*. That is because when you are here in your physical body you may have several missions during your life. Some people may only have one mission, but most people have more than one mission. These missions change over the course of your lifetime and also future lifetimes.

You decide on these missions before you come into this life and your guides and angels assist you in figuring out what missions you will accomplish to help you learn the lessons you have chosen to learn.

Sometimes the mission is about teaching other people rather than you learning a lesson. Some people even have missions to become a martyr or hero to inspire other humans. Some good examples of that would be Joan of Arc, Martin Luther King Jr. or Yeshua.

Other people may have one life mission or purpose to teach others. Another example of a life mission of teaching or being a martyr are children and babies who pass away from an illness or cancer or some other tragedy. During their brief incarnations on Earth, they teach so many lessons to their family, friends, neighbors, community and even the world. The most important things they are teaching are love, compassion and gratitude. This is Classroom Earth so every person who is here is learning lessons every day. Even dark souls are learning lessons.

My personal missions have changed several times in my lifetime and I currently have many missions, but my main purpose or mission in this body and life is to assist my brother and sister lightworkers with the Ascension of Earth. I am here to support the team, restore the balance and restore the feminine energies. I am also here to be of service to the planet (Mother Gaia), of service to people who need my help, and to hold the frequency of love and compassion for the planet and radiate that frequency out to every human and living creature.

If you are reading this book right now, you probably have a similar mission to be here for the Ascension of the planet and great awakening, since Starseeds have come here from all over the Universe for this event. This is Battlefield Earth and we are here to restore balance. Everyone here right now who is a love-based soul has a huge challenge ahead because of the demonic cabal reptilians who have been running this planet and enslaving humanity for thousands of years. It is a struggle to be here for many of us. A lot of lightworkers, starseeds and indigos are empathic and pick up all the energy of every living being, so it's difficult for us to be here. A lot of us have health issues, financial issue, relationship issues and other struggles and many of our issues are as a result of the dark entities running the planet. That is why we need to all support one another and stand together. Together we are strong, divided we fall.

When we talk about your life purposes or missions in your current body and incarnation, we are talking about both *spiritual* purposes and missions as well as *career* purposes and missions.

The career purposes can be anything from being a teacher in school, to being a stay at home mom and raising kids, to being a doctor and healing people. Your spiritual purposes could be similar to my own as I mentioned above, or they could be different. No matter what your purpose or mission might be, it is imperative that you are living your life with purpose, fulfilling that purpose and completing your missions. You have guardian angels to protect you so that you can fulfill your contract, missions and purposes, and you also have spirit guides to help guide you and advise you down your path.

Because you have free will, you are the one who has chosen all your experiences. Unfortunately, some people who are here were tricked into bad contracts of suffering by false light beings.

This all happened during our matrix prison lockdown which has recently been lifted from the planet. Future humans on Earth will not have to go through that type of thing. None of us had a life purpose to come here and suffer. We only have mass suffering on Earth because of the evil dark cabal that tricked us into it, as well as because of our own egos which create much of the suffering.

I will be talking about how your ego prevents you from being happy in your life, later in this book.

We are sovereign beings and our sovereignty was taken from us thousands of years ago, but we now have it back again. It is time for you to declare your sovereignty, to take back control over your destiny and co-create the life you want to have. Due to the energetic upgrades to this planet you are now able to manifest everything in your life much more easily and quickly than before. However, you need to be very careful with every one of your thoughts, as well as your speech and actions, because you are instantly manifesting.

Your journey is unique to you, so whatever mission or purpose you have is going to look completely different from everyone else's. Missions may seem the same from the outside, but all the intricacies of your life journey will be unique. The same thing applies to your soul journey. Please keep in mind that the amount of time it takes you to accomplish your missions and purpose is not important because the time it takes is different for each and every soul, and time only exists on Earth. In other dimensions and in the quantum field of energy there is no time. Your soul goes on forever.

You are not in a competition and all things will happen according to God's timing. Your missions will take as long as they are supposed to for benefit of your soul. You and God are cocreating and manifesting your life with every thought, word and action because of your free will and because you are the creator of your own personal experience.

God never gives you a *demand* and orders that you will go to Earth, live, marry, get into accidents, get sick, lose your job, become a famous star, etc. That is up to you to choose as your plan before you come into your body with your spirit guides and then you form a spiritual contract for this lifetime and every lifetime.

If you are unhappy with your contract you can always ask your guides and angels to help you break it, but it's not necessarily something you are supposed to do. Remember that before you came here you spent a lot of time figuring it all out.

There *are* some people on Earth who cannot fulfill their contracts, because they are just more than they can handle, and they ask for what is known as a "walk in". A "walk in" is another soul that takes your place and takes over all your memories in order to finish your life contract. This is especially important when leaving your family would cause a problem with *their* life contracts and missions. You also have exit doors written into your contract. Exit doors are times and situations where you can choose to die and go home. This is also something that is only good solution when your leaving is not going to harm other people or mess up other people's life plan.

If you do not know what your purpose is or you are not living purposefully, you will be unhappy in our life. Many people feel empty and lost in their lives because they don't know why they are here, or what purpose they have. More than 85% of people in the world are unhappy in their careers because their career is not fulfilling their purpose. It interferes with their happiness, health and even their relationships, and not knowing your purpose also affects you on a psychological level. It can also make you physically sick since emotional stress affects your health.

Thus, it is of the utmost importance to figure out why you are here and what your purposes or missions are, so that you can have the happy fulfilling life you deserve.

There are many ways to discover what your purpose is. The best way is to learn how to go within yourself through meditation and follow your own inner guidance. If you are able to develop your psychic abilities, you can also communicate with your angels and guides directly. Of course, you can also read lots of books and research different careers or subjects.

The most beneficial exercise guiding you towards knowing is to make a list of all the things you are good at or talented at, side-by-side with a list all of the things that you love or are interested in. Also, make a list of subjects or careers you are attracted to. When you analyze the information and follow your inner guidance, you can usually figure out your mission and purpose.

You may find it useful to work with a spiritual guide like myself or a life coach to assist you. My own primary focus is to teach people how to be their own gurus because you already have all the answers you need regarding your life and spirit within you, and you can also go straight to God. Prayer is a huge way to discover your purpose. You can pray for answers to what your mission is as well as ask for the right information, right person to show up, right situation, etc. For myself, daily prayer is the most important part of my life.

Chapter 6

Low Vibration: Your Biggest Block to Ascension

The key to Ascension is raising your vibration as high as possible. However, there are so many things on Earth outside of you that can lower your vibration. There are also many things within your control that you think, say or do, that can lower your vibration. The things that you do and say, along with the choices you make, are 100% within your control.

In this chapter I will review all the different variables that could currently be lowering your vibration, along with some that have the potential to lower your vibration. In chapter 7, I will cover how to *raise* your vibration and in chapter 8, I will cover how to protect yourself so you can maintain a high vibration.

Here are some of the many things that can lower your vibration and drain your energy:

1. **Emotional Stress** – According to scientific research, 98% of illness is caused by subconscious or conscious emotional stress and the other 2% is caused by epigenetically inherited illnesses caused by your ancestors' emotional stress. Emotional stress initially shows up in the energy body before entering your physical body and will stay in your energy body, lower your vibration and take your chakra energy centers out of balance until you heal the emotional stress and rebalance the energy. The biggest types of emotional stress that lower your vibration include any negative

feelings, anxiety, panic attacks, anger, grief, trauma and holding onto unforgiveness or holding grudges.

2. **Other types of stress** coming from physical stressors from work and other places, living situations, money issues, etc.

3. **Fear – (False Evidence Appearing Real)**. It is very human to have fears and some fear is absolutely necessary or else we would be killed: Consider, for example, being afraid of crossing the street without looking first, or being afraid of a grizzly bear. However, when you go further down the rabbit hole and focus on your fears — or you are afraid of *too many* things — then the fear will lower your vibration. Some of the lowest vibration people in our world are those who are fear based. When you learn to trust in God and the angels that protect you, then you can start releasing most of your fears and turn them all over to God. Don't let fear take control of your life and block your Ascension.

4. **Lying to yourself and others** or not speaking your truth.

5. **Bad behavior and bad attitude** – This includes; being superficial or fake, acting mean, nasty, rude, jealous, disrespectful, possessive, egotistical and others. Ego related negative thoughts, attitudes, and behaviors will always lower your vibration. As my sister always says, "Don't be shitty!"

6. **Being an empath** and taking on the energies of other people and the planet. Most starseeds, lightworkers, and people with psychic or intuitive abilities are empaths and the empathic ability can suck your energy. You have to protect yourself.

7. **Negative thinking**, negative self-talk and negative or wrong beliefs. (I like to call it stinking thinking)

8. **Watching violent sports like boxing or MMA** – You may love this stuff, but every time you watch it, you are lowering your vibration. Accordingly, you need to choose what is more important, a healthy body/mind/spirit or watching violent sports. I know which one I would choose, and it doesn't involve guys beating on each other.

9. **Watching violent crime based TV shows and movies,** or horror films with blood and gore and violent scenes.

10. **Saying negative things out of your mouth** – Your thoughts and words are energy but your speech is the most powerful energy because sound is what created the universe so the sound coming out of your mouth can be used for good or bad. Your words are spells (spelling).

11. **Arguing, fighting and negative speech** – Every time you argue or fight with someone, your vibration is lowered. Watching others argue and fight also lowers vibration. Get relationship counseling if this is a problem in your life.

12. **Past life traumatic stress or past life Karma** – Even though most people have no clue that they have past life trauma or bad karma, these things can still be within you and lowering your vibration.

   If you do not have the intuitive ability to ask your guides and angels or your higher self if you have this and learn the details about it, then you will need to have someone help you diagnose the trauma and karma, and then help you clear and heal it. This is one of the many topics I work on with my clients. You can work with a shaman, healer, hypnotherapist or spiritual teacher. I have personally cleared my own past life traumas and karma with my own ability to get answers from my guidance team, along with prayer, working with a Body Talk practitioner and my two intuitive counselors.

13. **<u>Eating a poor diet</u>** – Everything you put into your mouth, whether it's a food, supplement, beverage or drug, vibrates at either a high vibration, a neutral vibration or a low vibration. Accordingly, everything that goes into your mouth has the ability to change your vibration in either a positive, or a negative way. In addition, everything that goes into your mouth has an impact on your physical health.

Since your body is the temple of your Holy Spirit as well as the Holy Spirit of God, and you only have one body, it is very important for you to take care of it by eating healthy and high vibration food and beverages, while staying away from things that lower your vibration.

Here is the breakdown of some of the foods and things you put into your mouth that lower your vibration. In the next chapter we will discuss the foods and beverages that *raise* your vibration.

Low vibrational foods and beverages:

- Soda pop
- Juice with added processed sugar
- BBQ foods
- Red meat
- Processed foods

- Fast food
- Fried foods
- Hydrogenated oils and fats
- Processed sugar and any foods sweets or desserts made with processed added sugars
- Chemicals, additives and preservatives – The worst ones are MSG, Propyl Gallate, Sulfites, Brominated Oils, Propylene Glycol, Carboxymethylcellulose, Mono-Glycerides and Di-Glycerides, Sodium Nitrate, Maleic Hydrazide,
  Bromates, Citric Acid (Made Using Sulfuric Acid) and Benzoates, Trans fats, Hydrogenated oils, Artificial food colors, High fructose corn syrup (HFCS), dextrose, Aspartame, Butylated hydroxyanisole (BHA) and butylated hydroxytoluene (BHT).
- Water that has fluoride and chlorine and other chemicals added
- Gluten
- Soy – Soy is mostly GMO with pesticides, plus soy causes 30 types of cancer and thyroid disorder. Organic fermented soy is better for you but still not particularly beneficial.
- Peanuts – Cause allergies for many people. Tend to be mostly GMO and carry micotoxins plus they are a lectin which is not good.
- Corn – Corn crops in US, Mexico and Canada are GMO

14. **Narcotic drugs, alcohol abuse or cigarettes** – The type of drugs that lower your vibration are drugs like LSD, Meth, Cocaine, Opioids, Heroin, etc. Certain plant medicines, like cannabis, do not lower your vibration. Alcohol in moderation will not lower your vibration, but too much alcohol *will* harm your body and your vibration. When you choose to harm your own body with substances that are not good for it, you are lowering your vibration because your body is the

"temple of the Holy Spirit". You could view as a bit like breaking your contract. Cigarettes and chewing tobacco may come from a plant but they are also harmful for your body. In addition, when you are under the influence of drugs, where you do not have 100% control over your mind and body, you can be taken over by demonic and other entities.

15. **<u>GMO's, toxins, heavy metals, pesticides and chemicals</u>** – These are found in numerous foods & beverages, in the environment, personal care items, air, clothes, home, and work.

16. **<u>Chemtrails</u>** – Anyone who is awake — and even people who are not awake — have seen airplanes spray chemicals all over the world every day in the form of chemtrails, especially in the USA. You can sit outside your home and watch these planes release these chemtrails in a checkerboard pattern or as hundreds of diagonal lines overhead. These chemtrails contain aluminum, barium, mercury, and other harmful substances. Nobody seems to know exactly *who* is spraying them and there are many stories floating around about *why* they are being sprayed, but the fact is that they are not good for humans, animals or the environment.

17. **<u>Fluorescent lighting</u>** – This type of lighting puts out very strong EMFs which are harmful to your energy body, brain and to your physical body

18. **<u>Negative energy vampires</u>** – These are the people who are always negative, mean, rude, disrespectful, etc. Many of us have friends, family, neighbors and coworkers who operate like this.

19. **Bad EMF's & radiation from cell phones**, cell towers, electric towers, computers, machinery, equipment, electronic devices of any kind, smart meters, electrical wiring, dirty electricity, microwave ovens & other similar emissions.

20. **Demonic attack** – Unfortunately, there are demons on Earth, and they like to attack humans because they work for Satan and their main directive is to destroy us. If a demon attacks you, you will not only have your vibration lowered, but you may feel it physically and mentally too. Most people do not know they are being attacked by a demon.

21. **Psychic attack** perpetrated by people using dark magic, witchcraft, voodoo or their psychic abilities.

22. **O.D.B.'s (Other Dimensional Beings)** – shadow people, ghosts, restless spirits, E.T.s and other entities.

23. **Being in crowded places** (shopping malls, concerts, airports, etc.) where the energy tends to be intense and chaotic.

24. **Transportation** — Airplanes, buses, cars and trains.

Chapter 7

High Vibration: Your Key to a Happy Ascension

The most important key to your Ascension is to maintain a very high vibration at all times.

That may seem difficult to do. However, it's not that difficult if you follow some of the suggestions that I am about to offer you here. If you decide you need more help, I would be happy to give you a private session to help you raise your vibration.

Here are some of the many ways in which you can raise your vibration. There are actually numerous books about how to raise your vibration, and some of them offer more than 100 methods.

In this book I am only covering what I think are the most important methods, based on channeled information, as well as on my own years of experience trying out many different approaches on myself. Please keep in mind that it is very important to work on improving yourself every single day of your life. Raising your vibration is not a temporary thing, it's a lifelong commitment because you will always be faced with things that lower your vibration.

1. **Practice self-love** — Look deeply at yourself and within yourself and learn to accept and love yourself just the way you are, with all your issues and problems. No human is perfect. We are all unique and we all have flaws but God doesn't care about our flaws. See yourself the way God sees you. God loves you unconditionally and sees you as a beautiful divine

spirit. You cannot fully and properly love other people if you do not love yourself first.

2. **Practice daily gratitude** — Gratitude is a feeling that is of the highest vibration. Every time you feel grateful or show your gratitude you are raising your vibration. You can do a gratitude prayer, or keep a journal or just feel grateful, but you should do this daily.

3. **Create happiness and joy in your life** by doing something every day that gives you joy or makes you happy. Your vibration is always higher when you are happy. Later in this book you will read about how to create a happy life.

4. **Do not lie** — Be fully honest with yourself and everyone else at all times because if you lie to yourself about anything it lowers your vibration. Stand in your truth and speak your truth.

5. **Learn how to conquer your emotional stress** – Stress management is the most important thing you can do to ensure a long, healthy and happy life. Always claim, own, and feel your feelings; do not ignore them and stuff them. Learn how to fully process your emotions like grief, sadness, anger and fear. Always claim your emotional baggage and heal all your wounds. Work on peeling away all the layers of the emotional onion and bring everything up to the surface to be cleared and healed.

This is an ongoing process that could take months, years and a lifetime but you constantly have to be working on yourself. When we allow our body, mind and spirit to become weighed down by negative emotions, trauma and other mental garbage, it lowers our vibration. You can also work with a mental health counselor, minister, healer or life coach to help you with healing emotional stress.

6. **<u>Get help with clearing and healing emotional trauma</u>** from this life and past lifetimes.

7. **<u>Clear and remove any blocks</u>** you have that are the result of karma, curses, contracts and vows. Many people have bad karma that lower their vibration and some people took vows of poverty in past lifetimes that keep them stuck in poverty in *this* lifetime.

8. **<u>Focus your mind on positive thoughts always</u>**. If a negative thought comes up, immediately refocus on something positive. The longer you focus on the negative thoughts, the more your vibration is lowered, however if you counteract your negative thoughts quickly with a positive mantra or thought then it will not have a chance to harm you.

9. **<u>Eat a very healthy, high vibration diet.</u>** You can raise the vibration of your food and beverages by praying over them or blessing them. You can also place your food or beverages on top of a Tesla purple plate, a crystal plate or an orgonite plate to charge it and raise the vibration. You can even place your grocery bags on top of these tools to raise the vibration of the food you buy. Some healthy high vibration foods and beverages include:

   • Fruits and vegetables – especially dark leafy greens like kale and superfruits and berries
   • Fresh squeezed juices and Green juice
   • Sprouts
   • Raw and living foods
   • Nuts and seeds

- Fermented foods – kimchi, yoghurt, kefir, kombucha, sauerkraut
- Purified mineral water or alkaline water – (fluoride and chlorine removed)
- Raw Cacao (raw chocolate)
- Organic herbal teas
- Himalayan salt and sea salt
- Organic foods

10. **Drink plenty of purified water** daily that you have blessed and/or charged. You can use orgonite to charge your water and your foods.

11. **Practice daily meditation and mindfulness** – This is one of the best ways to raise your vibration very quickly. I have been meditating for over 20 years and it helped me so much that I went back to college a decade ago to get certified to teach meditation and mindfulness. If you need help learning how to meditate, I would be happy to help you.

12. **Essential oils** like Frankincense, Myrrh, Palo Santo and sage can clear out any negative energy and help keep your vibration high. These are the highest vibration of all the essential oils. There are many other high vibration oils you can use daily and they have wonderful scents. Be careful with essential oils, however, and test for allergies, because some people are sensitive and the oils are super powerful.

13. **Practice mantras to raise your vibration**. Some of my favorite mantras:
"I am love and light"
"I am the truth the light and the way"
"I am healthy, happy and prosperous"

14. **Do some type of Yoga, Qi-Gong, Tai Chi** or breathwork as often as possible. Kundalini work is also great and very beneficial.

15. **Practice Spirituality and prayer** – Taking time to connect with God and your higher-self on a daily basis is one of the most important ways to raise your vibration. Prayer will always raise your vibration. Setting up a daily spiritual practice that is meaningful to you is a great way to raise your vibration. Spirituality is not the same as religion. Spirituality is your personal practice that improves your relationship with God, the universe and your own higher self and soul. You do not need to practice a religion nor go to a church or synagogue in order to be spiritual or to pray. However, you *can* do both at same time. You can talk to God anywhere you are. Some people have an altar in their home where they pray. Some people read the Bible or another spiritual book daily. There are many ways you can do this, but it's a personal choice and there is no right or wrong way; it's all about what feels good for you and what helps you to connect with God.

16. **Exercise daily** — Exercise is a great way to raise your vibration. Make sure to pick a type of exercise that is fun for you. If you get bored, you will not keep up with an exercise routine. Also do not do exercise that is too hard for you because you can injure your body. Make sure you always start out with gentle exercise and work your way up to more intense exercise if your body is able.

17. **Get at least 7 to 8 hours of sleep every night**. This is your battery recharger. Lack of sleep = lack of energy = lower vibration.

18. **Watch uplifting, motivational, spiritual, or educational TV** shows, videos and movies.

19. **Watch or listen to comedy**. Try to laugh as much as possible. Remember the saying "Laughter is the best medicine?"

20. **Only hang out with like-minded, positive, uplifting, supportive and loving people**. The people you hang out with can either raise or lower your vibration based on how high or low their vibration is.

21. **Use crystals to raise your vibration** – We have many natural tools and medicines on this planet that were created by God for our healing and assistance. All crystals and rocks have different vibrational frequencies that can protect you and raise your vibration as well as assist you with healing.

    There are some crystals that have energies that are harmful, so you it is wise to learn about which types of crystals are best to use, and how to clear them, program them and use them. There are many types of crystals you can use to raise your vibration by wearing them on our body, placing them in a pocket, putting them under your bed or anywhere in your home. The best books to buy to learn more about crystals are "The Crystal Bible 1" and "The Crystal Bible 2." These books will help you determine which crystals to use to raise your vibration. One of the highest vibration crystals is quartz, but be careful with them, because they amplify energy.

22. **Do regular Reiki or Chakra clearing and Balancing sessions** – During my lifetimes I have learned many different types of energy work and

Reiki, Qi Gong and Chakra Balancing are my favorites that I use regularly. I teach a Chakra Balancing and healing class and also offer private chakra sessions.

23. **Spend time in nature** – Gardening, sitting on the grass, or practicing Earthing are beneficial. Earthing is when you walk outside and stand or walk with your bare feet on the grass or sand, or put your back up against a tree. In Japan they practice something called "Forest Bathing" where you walk through the forest and take in all the smells, sights and sounds.

24. **Spend time near waterfalls, the ocean, beaches, rivers or lakes**. Water is healing and the negative ions from waterfalls, river rapids and ocean waves are healing and raise your vibration.

25. **Take classes and seminars** in metaphysics, spirituality or any type of education that expands your mind and spirit. Alternately, read books on the subjects that feed your soul. When you engage in these activities you are raising your vibration.

26. **Spend time around pets or animals** because they vibrate at the frequency of 100% unconditional love. Horses have exceptionally high vibration but so do dogs and cats.

27. **Help people or do service for other people** – Every time we help someone or serve the greater good, we are raising our vibration.

28. **Listen to high vibration music**: Buddhist and Hindu chants, Native American flute music, Benedictine chants, St. Hildegard Von Bingen's music, meditation music and Solfeggio frequencies. The best

type to listen to is the frequency of love 528 HZ but there are others that are fantastic.

29. **Sing, chant or tone**. (Most spiritual tone to sing is "Ah" or "Om")

30. **Do some drumming** on a Native American Elk skin drum or join a drumming circle. I use my elk skin drum to clear my energy and to do shamanic work.

31. **Use Tuning forks or Tibetan Singing bowls**.

32. **Do some work with the Ascended Masters**. You will learn more about this later in this book.

33. **Put Himalayan salt crystal lamps all over your home** and make sure they are turned on and get warm for a while to release the negative ions, which offer similar benefits to sitting by a waterfall. Sprinkle Himalayan salt into your water when you drink (as long as you don't have a high blood pressure issue, if so, then do not use salt in your food or drinks)

34. **Clear your energy after being exposed to people or places that lower your vibration**. Learn how to do it yourself or hire someone to do it for you. It only takes a few minutes to clear your energy.

35. **Do inner child work to heal any trauma you had as a child**. Most of us experienced some sort of trauma as children, either from our family, strangers, school bullies, accidents, and other things. Healing your inner child is very important for Ascension.

36. **Forgive everyone in your life who has every hurt you** by practicing Ho'oponopono, which is a

Hawaiian chant and practice of reconciliation and forgiveness. The Hawaiian word translates into English simply as "correction".

37. **Spend time with friends or family who are high vibration** and make you feel happy.
Take care of your "Temple of the Holy spirit" – Besides eating healthy high vibration food, you should always be practicing self-care. Simple things like getting a pedicure, taking a bubble bath, sitting in a hot tub, getting a massage, having sex with someone you love and other pleasureable experiences are all beneficial.

38. **Spend time in a garden around flowers and plants** – Plants, trees and flowers are some of the highest vibration organisms on Earth. Go spend some time digging in Mother Earth Gaia, planting a veggie, fruit or flower garden and tending to it. This will bring happiness and rais your vibration. You will be able to create a close connection with the love frequency of our Mother Gaia.

Chapter 8

Clearing, Balancing and Protecting Your Energy

Although we are talking about your energy, the recommendations I am about to give you here may also work on clearing, cleansing and protecting your physical body, astral body, spirit body, etheric body and the other bodies that make up who you are.

First, I would like to go over methods for testing your energy for holes, blocks, and unbalances.

Energy testing methods:

- Muscle testing or kinesiology – You can do this yourself, have a friend help you, or visit a chiropractor, N.D. or other doctor who is also a kinesiologist to do it for you. I also use this technique on myself and clients. Entire books have been written on the topic of kinesiology, so you will need to research it or consult with someone like myself to teach you how to do it.

- See a Chinese medicine doctor or acupuncturist – Chinese medicine and acupuncture is based on your energy meridians. By doing specific tests and asking you a series of questions, these doctors can tell you which part of your energy body is out of balance.

- If you are intuitive, psychic, or clairvoyant, you can ask your higher-self or your spirit guides what is out of balance or has blocks.

- Use a Rife device or other device made in Germany and Europe that tests your energy. There are several new types of equipment out to do energy testing. Naturopathic doctors or holistic doctors will usually have this type of equipment.

- Thermographic scanners – These can be used on your entire body to scan for energy problems. However, these are becoming very popular devices to screen for breast cancer. Illnesses like cancers show up in the energy body before they show up in the physical body. Doctors are able to see hot spots where you may be starting to form a cancer or illness, or where illnesses will happen in near future if you don't make major health changes. Unfortunately, energy testing equipment is not yet covered by insurance companies. Additionally, allopathic doctors do not use this type of highly innovative preventative equipment and most have no clue
what they are. If you want to get one of these scans you will need to see a naturopathic doctor, holistic doctor, integrative medicine doctor or functional medicine doctor.

- Pendulum – This is one of my favorite methods for testing my own energy, as well as my clients'. You can buy them from any metaphysical, spiritual, or crystal shop, or you can make your own simply by tying a string to a ring. My personal favorites are copper pendulums and quartz crystal pendulums. Look these up on the Internet and you will find thousands of different types to choose from. If you can buy a pendulum in person, you will be able to hold it in your hand and see whether the energy of the pendulum you pick out is right for you. Make sure to cleanse and bless any pendulum you buy from a store so that it has good energy for you. When other people handle your energy tools, they leave their energy on them, so they need to be cleansed and blessed.

- Mind/body Connection – The quickest and easiest way to know if you have blockages or imbalances in your energy or chakras is to pay attention to your health. Work on improving your mind body connection. When you can tell that there is something off or wrong in your physical body, you can always link it to imbalances, blocks or problems in your energy body. Whenever you are blocked or unbalanced, you will have a mental or physical symptom or problem. This is something I cover in my chakra balancing and healing seminars, as well as in one on one sessions with clients.

Methods for clearing, balancing and healing your energy body:

You will probably notice that some of the items on this list were mentioned in the section on how to raise your vibrational frequency. Raising your overall vibration and healing holes, blocks and imbalances in your energy or chakras are different things, but some of same methods are used.

- Crystals, rocks, gemstones – There are many types of crystals, rocks, and gemstones you can use to clear, balance, and heal your energy body. Sometimes they can heal your physical body as well. All crystals, rocks and gemstones are part of Mother Gaia and they all vibrate at a different energy frequency.

  When you pick out and use these tools, it is important for you to choose those that are specific for the purpose and that resonate with your energy.

Sometimes there will be a specific purpose — for example, clearing emotional anger — and there wi several different crystals, gems and rocks that wil work for that particular purpose. It will be up to you to pick the ones that you resonate with or feel drawn too.

I highly recommend that you purchase books on how to clear and program crystals, gems and rocks for healing. These books also tell you which ones to pick out for different emotions or health problems. The two books I like best are "The Crystal Bible 1" and "The Crystal Bible 2" by Judy Hall. Not everything would fit in one book, so there are two books. I have had the greatest success following the advice in these books.

If you want help figuring out which crystals to use, how to clear and program them and how to use them, please feel free to contact me. I have been collecting crystals and rocks since I was three years old, due to my past lifetimes in Atlantis and Lemuria where they were used as an integral part of the culture. In fact, some people who are obsessed with crystals and rocks and collect them in this lifetime were living in Atlantis in a past lifetime and that is why they love crystals so much. Later on in the book I will tell you which crystals are best for grounding and protecting your energy field.

- Use Himalayan pink salt or Celtic sea salt – You can put a pinch of these in your water and drink it to clear your energy and additionally get a nice dose of trace minerals, or you can soak in a bathtub with either one. You can also put Himalayan salt crystal lamps or candle holders around your house in as many rooms as possible. Best places would be in your bedroom and office. When you heat up the lamps or candle holders they emit negative ions which help clear your energy, protect you from electro-smog, EMFs and radiation and also give you the same feeling and health benefits as you get from being near a waterfall, the ocean or river rapids.

- Essential Oils – I love using oils to clear and balance energy. They have wonderful scents and there many types to choose from. You can either use them with a diffuser as aromatherapy, or you can mix the essential oil with a carrier oil and use it directly on your skin over each of your chakras. Some of my favorite oils include lavender, sage and palo santo. I also like "Valor" by Young Living. Research essential oils before doing this, buy organic only and make sure to avoid anything you know you are allergic to. If you have an allergic reaction to anything, please stop immediately and seek medical attention.

- Burn sage or palo santo and use it to smudge yourself. If you don't like burning things, you can make a smudging spray with oils and distilled water. You will want to smudge your home, office or car once in a while to clear negative energy and entities. If someone negative comes into your home, always smudge after they leave. If you have negative family members living with you, or negative roommates, then smudge regularly to keep the energy clear and the vibe high. Smudge yourself after you have been exposed to low vibration people, after you go to hospitals, medical centers, nursing homes or places where there are sick people or death. Also smudge yourself if you go anywhere you believe is haunted or has demonic activity, or if you are concerned that you may have picked up entity attachments when you were out in the world.

- Prayer and intention – If you want to clear, heal, balance or protect your energy you can pray and ask God, your guardian angels, archangels, spirit guides and Ascended Masters to help you to do so. You can also just use your intention to do the same.

- Sound Healing – The universe was created by sound. Many people — and Buddhists in particular — believe that the sound that created the universe and resonates with the energy of source creator is "OM". Sound and music can heal your body and it can also harm your body. If you listen to music or sounds that are in the wrong frequency, it can make you sick and even kill you. However, there are many types of sounds you can use to heal. My favorite sound healing methods include Tibetan Singing bowls; tuning forks; listening to 432 Hz, 528 Hz or other solfeggio frequency music; binaural beats music; drumming; chanting/singing or toning with voice; singing do, re, mi, fa, so, la, ti, do, listening to soothing meditation music or classical music.

- Practice Qi Gong, Tai Chi, or Yoga – These are all mind/body/spirit techniques that will help you keep your energy cleared and balanced and helps you to heal your physical body too.

- Energy healing techniques - Quantum Touch, Reiki, Chakra Balancing, Reconnective Healing, Pranic Healing, Pure Awareness Healing, Body Talk, Acupuncture, Remote Scalar Healing and numerous other energy healing techniques are available to help you.

- Emotional healing techniques – My favorites are The Healing Codes, Emotion Codes, Psych-K and Body Talk.

- Color therapy – You can use chakra colors to heal and balance your energy. You can wear the colors on your body, have them around you, meditate or gaze upon them, decorate your home or office with specific chakra colors, or eat foods with specific chakra colors.

- Bach Flower Remedies – These were created by Edward Bach, a British Homeopath in the year 1930. He discovered that flowers each have a special vibrational frequency that can be used for healing the emotional and physical body.

- Earthing – Walking barefoot on the grass or on a sandy beach helps you connect and ground your energy with Mother Gaia (Earth). It is important to do this once every day if possible. You can also put your back up against a tree or sit on the ground and meditate.

- Forest Bathing – the Japanese have done this for a very long time. When you walk through the forest or spend time in nature it helps you ground yourself and clear your energy. It is also very healing for the mental, emotional and physical bodies.

- Negative Ion water therapy. Sitting by a waterfall, river, ocean waves.

Energy Protection & grounding tools:

With all the crazy stuff we are all going through on Earth right now, along with all the EMFs, electro-smog, radiation, negative low vibe humans, demonic entities, disembodied spirits, negative ETs, archons and other things we have to deal with, it's important for you to stay grounded and to protect yourself, your home, office, and vehicles at all times.

It is especially important to ground yourself when you are doing any healing or energy work on other people, when you meditate, and when you are around large groups of strangers. If you are an empath like me, you will have to remain particularly vigilant about grounding and protecting yourself at all times. There are numerous ways to protect your energy body and ground yourself to the Earth. I am going to cover all the methods that I have had personal experiences with.

- Each day when you wake up and/or before you go to sleep at night, say an energy protection prayer and ask God, your guardian angels and Archangel Michael for protection. Also, ask for protection when you get into any vehicle for transportation, when you travel and when you go to public places. Finally, ask for your home and office to be protected.

- Energy protection crystals. You can wear the crystals on a necklace, bracelet or ring, carry them in your pocket or purse, place them near your computer, tape them to your cell phone or other devices, and place them in grids around your home, office and car to protect your energy field. These tools make you stronger when you use the right ones and their energy will create a barrier of protection.

  The types most commonly recommended for energy protection are: Himalayan salt crystals and lamps, black tourmaline crystals, black onyx, lapis lazuli, turquoise, blue kyanite, black obsidian, golden sheen obsidian, amethyst, labradorite, staurolite faerie cross, shungite, orgonite, smokey quartz, selenite and apache tear.

The Egyptians, Persians, Chinese, Tibetans, Aztecs and Incas of South America, along with Native North Americans have all used turquoise and lapis lazuli to protect themselves from evil. The three protection stones I personally carry at all times are black tourmaline, selenite and shungite. Shungite and blue kyanite will protect you from cell phones, WiFi, computer and electro smog, EMFs and radiation. Selenite clears away all negative and low vibrational energy and protects you. Black tourmaline and smokey quartz are great for protection against entities, low vibration people and psychic attack. Sodalite, Himalayan Salt lamps and Kyanite are great stones to place near your computer to absorb and disperse some of the radiation and EMFs. Protect your entire living space by creating crystal grids in your home. I like to place Selenite pillars in each of the four corners of the house and then I also have special grids throughout our rooms to anchor in high vibrational grounding energies from Gaia.

- You can also use crystals to ground yourself. My favorite crystal for grounding is hematite. Other good grounding crystals are black onyx, red jasper and black tourmaline.

- Stay away from negative energy vampires; get rid of bad relationships – This is one of the best ways to protect your energy. As I have personally made my way through this Ascension process, I have gotten rid of many long-time "friends" who were sucking my energy and making me sick. I also stopped speaking to certain family members who were having the same effect on me. It is difficult to part ways with people, especially family members or friends you have known for a long time, but when you love and respect yourself fully it becomes easier.

Our time in these bodies is short, and it's important to keep your life full of happiness and joy, instead of strife, pain, and sorrow. When you are surrounded by fear-based negative people, it sucks and lowers your energy and makes you physically and mentally sick. In the past, I have actually changed jobs to get away from negative people who were making me sick. I don't recommend you just up and quit your job to escape negative energy-draining people, however, if you can find another equal or better job and then quit, then that would be very beneficial for you.

- Learn protection and grounding meditations, as well as visualization and breathing exercises, and use them before you enter crowded places, meetings, or go near people you know are negative. I have been teaching these tools to my clients for over a decade.

- Put a Himalayan Salt Crystal Lamp in every room — as I mentioned earlier — especially next to your computer to disperse the EMFs and radiation from equipment and the WiFi.

- Essential Oils – There are specific oils and oil blends you can use for protection and grounding. Earlier I mentioned Palo Santo for smudging and clearing energy but it can also be used to protect you. Since I am an empath, I like to dab a little Palo Santo on each of my chakras before I go to a mall or similar place with a lot of people. I also will dab a little on me before bedtime to protect my body and spirit when I am in the dream state.

- Bless everything you eat, drink, or take (pills), before putting it in your mouth. You can charge your water and beverages with love and healing by praying over them and speaking Love into the water. I recommend reading about Dr. Masaru Emoto's water experiments to learn more. You can heal water with love and actually change the water molecules just by using love.

- Stand away from microwave ovens and minimize cooking with them since they harm your energy and your physical body.

- Avoid keeping your cell phone against your body for long periods of time. In general, minimize cell phone use as much as possible or use phone on speaker phone or with a head set to keep the negative frequencies away from your brain and body. Also, try to stay away from cell phone towers. Do not buy a home near electrical towers or power stations since they damage your energy field and your body.

- There are special chips, buttons, plates, electrical plug devices and other protection devices you can purchase on the Internet to attach to your cell phone, install in your home, and use with a computer to protect you from electro smog. There are even plates you can use under a glass of water or food to raise its vibration. Before you buy these things, make sure you thoroughly research and check out the ratings and testimonials from actual users because there are many of these products that are overpriced worthless scams.

Chapter 9

Why do We Get Sick and Die?

In 1986 I got very sick with pain in my gallbladder, and none of the doctors I saw could determine what was wrong with me, despite running a multitude of tests. After a lot of research and inner work, I realized that I had had an allergic reaction that caused my gallbladder to swell up with inflammation. However, none of the doctors could figure that out.

In 1987 I was misdiagnosed by a doctor who could have killed me, and might have, were it not for the fact that I was an intuitive and felt that I was being misdiagnosed and given wrong information. My mother sent me to her doctor for a second opinion and that doctor confirmed to me that the first doctor had truly misdiagnosed me. She told me that if I were to have taken the drug the first doctor handed me, I could have gotten extremely ill and possibly died.

After those two incidents, I realized that doctors call their business a "practice" because they are practicing on their patients. They do not know all the answers and harm people with misdiagnoses, dangerous medical mistakes, along with prescribing drugs that cause side effects and possibly even death. Many allopathic doctors break their Hippocratic Oath on a daily basis. I have watched many family members and friends die at the hands of this corrupt cabal-run medical system. I wish those family members and friends would have listened to me when I advised them to seek alternative, holistic and natural medicine doctors and treatments.

I also realized that the entire medical system is broken, and it was up to me to become empowered and responsible for my own health since I could not depend on allopathic medicine or doctors for healing. The entire allopathic medical industry is ruled by the big pharma cabal and is basically a system rooted in waiting for you to get sick and then put a band-aid on your symptoms with their toxic lab created drugs. The longer they keep you sick, the more money they make.

There are 100s of cures for cancer, but the big pharma companies will not let them see the light of day. In fact, a friend of mine was actually present in the board room of a major pharmaceutical company when the CEO told the Board of Directors that he would never let cancer cures see the light of day.

The situation is so bad that all the scientists and doctors who have created cancer cures and have healed their patients have either had their licenses to practice medicine revoked, or those doctors and scientists have died or disappeared under mysterious circumstances.

Many years ago, I was working for a Naturopathic doctor who was curing 100s of patients with cancer. Someone reported him to the state medical board, and they took away his license to practice and threatened him and his family's lives if he continued to help people with cancer.

Since this is a book about Ascension, it is important to mention that this beautiful Mother Gaia that we live on was created with many natural plant medicine cures and other cures waiting for us to utilize. There are even healing elements in the rocks and earth. The best healing comes from energy and nature. When you take lab created big pharma drugs, you are lowering your vibration. Of course, you need to do what is best for *you* and if you have certain health conditions where you have to take drugs to stay alive, then it's important for you to do so. I am just here sharing my truth.

Since 1986 and my being let down by the big pharma run allopathic medical industry, I have been studying, reading, and learning everything I can about how to heal the body and mind. I have had to heal myself over and over for 30 plus years. I have also been working with alternative, holistic and natural medicine practitioners for three decades, since they use a functional approach to diagnosing the root cause of your health problem and then they work with you to heal your body.

Allopathic medicine doctors will try to diagnose you and if they come up with some diagnosis, their options are typically surgery, drugs or rehab. The drugs have hundreds of side effects including death and do not *cure* disease. The only drugs that can cure you are antibiotics or antivirals and that is only in the case of bacterial infections and certain viruses. If you want to *heal* your body, then you need natural holistic medicine. After learning a lifetime of health information, I founded and ran a healing and health coaching business from February of 2011 until the end of 2018. I even wrote a bestselling health book that I unfortunately had to remove from the market when I shut down my health coaching and healing business. Sadly, I was not able to earn enough money to pay the bills.

For many years, I have been questioning why I was getting sick and why other people get sick. Furthermore, ever since I was a small child, I developed a terrible fear of death. When I would think about it and wonder what happens after I die, I would have panic attacks. For most of my life I questioned why people die and was terrified until I had a few or more near-death experiences.

Those near-death experiences happened when I was pregnant with my second child and after I gave birth to her. After having my kids, I had a huge kundalini experience that blew my third eye wide open and I developed numerous psychic and other abilities on top of the ones I was born with. Some of these abilities included the ability to see and hear people who had passed away. I also developed the ability to hear and see my spirit guides, angels, Ascended Masters, God, and certain star beings (E.T.s). Following those experiences, I never feared death ever again. However, I still kept asking "*why do people die?*" and never got an answer. About ten years ago — when I started really channeling Yeshua and Mary Magdalene, as well as Mother/Father God — I started getting answers to my questions about death.

Recently when I started channeling this book, I also got the answers to the question of why we all get sick and have mental and physical health problems. I waited 30 plus years to finally receive this information. I guess I was finally ready for it!

We tend to receive important information when we are ready for it. In this chapter I will be sharing with you all the information I have channeled about illness and death. If you are like me, you will probably have a big "aha" moment and everything will make sense to you. However, if it still doesn't make sense or you do not agree, don't worry, because your truth will come to you when you are ready.

What follows is a list of reasons why you and I have mental and physical health problems. Each of us have at least one or more of these. Some of us might have all of them. If you are not sure why you have your health issues, or which ones of these apply to you, it's important for you to work with a medical intuitive like myself, a psychic, a medium or a shaman to help you find clarity.

1. Not taking care of your "Temple of the Holy Spirit," aka Accountability – If you remember, part of the definition of Ascension is being able to step into accountability and always be accountable for your actions. Many humans do not take care of their bodies. They either eat a bad diet, or they do not exercise, or they smoke, drink, take drugs, don't sleep enough, have an unhealthy lifestyle and do other things that are abusive to the human body. A large

number of people in the United States are obese, unhealthy, have high blood pressure, heart disease and diabetes due to horrible dietary habits and lifestyle.

You have 100% control over taking care of your body. No one will do this for you. It is up to you to take care of yourself. People who do the previously mentioned negative things to their bodies are lowering their vibration. Part of raising your vibration is taking care of your "temple". This means eating a good diet, getting adequate amounts of sleep and exercise, and not drinking, eating or taking anything harmful into your body.

2. Mental and physical health problems are just part of the Ascension process and being in a human body. Once you agreed to incarnate into a physical human body on Earth, you accepted becoming vulnerable to illness. We are not robots and we are not impervious to mental or physical sickness. There are a few lucky people I have met who have never been sick in their entire life. It may be that they have amazing genetics. I have met a few people who have extraterrestrial implants in their body that protect them from ever getting sick. I would personally love something like that since I have had a lifetime of suffering with health issues.

3. Ascension symptoms can cause many problems for most of us on a physical, energetic, and mental level, especially those of us who are highly sensitive or empathic. I spoke about these Ascension symptoms previously in this book.

4. Lowering your density to come to Earth – Some of us come from much higher vibrational dimensions or densities and had to vibrationally lower ourselves

considerably to live on Earth in a human body. Some of us are angelic beings, star beings from other planets, Ascended Masters and even elementals. You may have been 8-10 feet tall before you came into your current body. I know some people who were faeries before incarnating as a human for this big Ascension event. When you have to change or lower your energy down to match the heavy 3rd density of Earth, it can create many problems in your human body, which is basically "reacting" to the low density. As the vibration of the planet gets higher, it will hopefully get easier for all of us.

5. Spiritual, psychic or demonic attack and black magic – There is a lot of dark energy on planet Earth, along with many dark beings. Some people experience mental and physical health problems as a result of having been attacked by these beings. If you are a lightworker, indigo, earth angel or starseed that has come here to usher in the Ascension and New Earth, then you may be a target of the darkness. The dark ones want to put out your light.

   However, you can do many things to protect yourself. I spoke about protection tools in the last chapter. Your biggest power is prayer. Asking your angels and Archangel Michael to protect you everywhere you go. Black tourmaline crystal and selenite are my go-to crystals that I take with me everywhere for this type of protection, along with saying my prayers and asking for protection.

   If you suspect someone or something is attacking you with dark magic, psychic power, negative energy, etc, please start praying immediately and ask for it to be stopped and prevented, and ask to be put into a bubble of protection with the armor of God. Then contact someone who is an expert in clearing this type of energy, and removing these blocks from you so you can fulfil your purpose here with peace, health and happiness.

6. Learning lessons – Some of your mental and physical health issues develop either for you to learn a lesson, or for you to be a teacher of lessons to others. I found out that many of the health issues I have had in my life were given to me for the purpose of being able to help other people as a healer. In fact, every healer I have ever met has been riddled with health problems. Many of their health issues were provided for their learning experience so they could turn around and help other humans to heal themselves.

7. Angelic intervention – Believe it or not, if your guardian angels need to prevent you from traveling somewhere — say, getting into your car or doing anything that may lead to your death — they can give you or one of your loved ones a simple health problem to keep you from doing whatever it was that would have endangered your life or the life of others. One such example would be if you come down with a mysterious upset stomach before you need to leave for an appointment. Another example: you sprain your ankle and are not able to go on a camping trip. Have you ever had strange mystery illnesses that happened right before you were supposed to go somewhere or do something? I have had this happen many times.

8. Experiences you wrote into your life contract – Some health issues may have been chosen by you to experience in this lifetime for various reasons. When you wrote up your life contract with your spirit guides and angels, you could have chosen to have some or all of your Earthly health experiences. Think of it as trying on different hats, shoes or maybe costumes in a play. You are trying on different experiences.

9. Some health issues can be caused by past life karma. Earlier in this book we talked about how karma used to be a thing until recently. Unfortunately, you if you were born before 2012, some of your past or current health problems may have been a result of karma. You can ask for God and the angels to clear these issues so you can heal and move on with your Earth mission. Releasing all your past karma is very important at this time. Unless you voluntarily release and heal your karma from past lifetimes, it will stay with you till the end of this lifetime.

10. Cabal created health issues – The dark cabal that has been running the planet for 10,000 years has been doing everything in their power to kill off all humans and make us suffer with all sorts of health issues. The dark entities feed off of your fear and suffering, so that when you are ill, they win. Some of the things they have done to our planet that are possibly making you sick right now include putting fluoride and other chemicals in our water; using poisonous pesticides and glyphosates on all the fruits, vegetables, grain crops and cotton crops; chemtrails in the skies; nanobots; toxic vaccinations; chemicals in the food; toxic prescription drugs with multiple side effects; weaponized foods; fast food; processed sugar; tobacco; hard street drugs; GMOs (genetically modified foods); cellphones; computers and other sources of EMFs and radiation; HARP, and a multitude of other things they do to humanity to shrink the population and keep us in a constant state of illness, fear and suffering.

11. Trauma and emotional stress from past lifetimes – If you had any trauma or emotional stress in past lifetimes that has not been cleared and healed, it can carry over into this lifetime and cause health

112

problems. Best thing to do is work with a healer to find out if you have this issue, then clear and heal it. Right now, during this Ascension, we are all having lots of past trauma come up for healing.

12. Being an empath – If you are empathic and sensitive to people and/or animals you can take on other people's emotional issues and health problems. In fact, if you are highly empathic and compassionate you can take on the problems of the entire world. This is an issue you need to deal with on a daily basis by saying protection prayers and engaging in other protection activities for yourself.

13. Demonic takeover – Some people have health problems because they have been taken over or possessed by demons, various entities, or negative E.T.s. This is particularly common with people who do a lot of hard drugs and alcohol. When you are under the influence of these substances, it is really easy for entities to take you over.

14. Wounds from wars in other dimensions – Some lightworkers, earth angels and starseeds go to other dimensions and planets while they are meditating or sleeping at night. In these realms they are fighting negative E.T.s or Demons. They may be getting wounded in battle and bring those wounds with them back into their bodies and then those wounds show up as mystery pain and illness.

15. Stress – According to doctors and researchers like Bruce H. Lipton, PhD, 98% of health problems are caused by emotional and other types of stress. I don't know if that percentage is true, but I do know that stress is very bad for your health. The American Medical Association says that 85% of health problems

are caused by stress. It is very important to prevent and manage your stress as well as possible.

16. Epigenetics – You may have inherited illnesses caused by trauma and stress inflicted on to your ancestors when they were here, and it was passed down to you through your DNA. A good example would be if your grandparent had a traumatic war experience, and as a result of that trauma not being healed they suffered from health problems, then those health problems are passed down to you through your DNA.

17. Tricked by false light beings – Many humans on Earth have been tricked into false contracts by dark entities masquerading as light beings. Some of this is related to the rat wheel of samsara, which is a false prison created by dark beings (basically reptilian Sith lords) to keep you trapped and suffering. These dark beings actually feed on the fear and suffering of humans, so they win when they can make many people sick. You can break these false contracts now that we are Ascending.

Reasons why people die too young

Although there are several reasons people die too young, please keep in mind that all human souls have free will and in the end it is up to us how, when and why we die. Because of the law of free will, no human can be killed without their agreement. However, some people may have died because they were tricked by dark entities into their agreement. We always have free will to choose but dark beings have influenced many people's choices for thousands of years.

These are the main reasons why people die too young or before their time:

1. Babies and children die because they are little martyrs and teachers. They are teaching their family, friends, neighbors, community and the world lessons of compassion, gratitude, love, forgiveness, and kindness when they get cancers and other illnesses and die, or when they are killed. It is always devastating when they die, but keep in mind that children and babies are pure souls and go straight to heaven. The people who are left behind experience the trauma and suffering of their loss, but the children are safe at home with our unconditional loving Creator.

2. Contract – You get to determine in your life plan or contract when you want to leave Earth and by what method. It's different for every person, based on what they want to learn or experience, or which role they are playing in someone else's experience. Unfortunately, as mentioned above, some people have been tricked into bad contracts and wind up leaving when they don't want to go or still have unfinished business. Many people have escape doors built into their life contract, so that if things on Earth get too difficult for them, they can leave. My father used one of his escape doors because his life was unfulfilled and unhappy, and he didn't want to deal with it anymore.

3. Learning and teaching – Some people die a specific way and at a certain age so that they can learn lessons and also teach lessons to the people around them.

4. Some people are killed by dark entities before it's their time. Some of those people may have

voluntarily elected to have this happen while others may have been tricked into it. The dark entities who do this are breaking universal codex and laws and will be held accountable for their crimes.

5. Karma – Up until recent years there was karma and some people would die as a result of past lifetime karma.

6. Cabal depopulation plan – A lot of people on Earth die younger than normal, due to all the things implemented by the dark cabal as part of their world depopulation plan. I outlined the things they do in the section on why people have illnesses.

7. Black or dark magic – Curses, plagues and dark magic are real and have been used by demonic entities and dark beings for thousands of years to harm and kill humans. Again, if someone dies as a result of this, it's because they either agreed to it or were tricked into it.

8. Trying on different experiences like playing a part in a play – Some people die at a certain age or have a certain type of death as part of their soul experience and journey of learning.

The good news is that because of this Ascension we are going through, all the false light beings, dark entities, dark cabal, negative ETs and others who have been committing crimes against humanity, will all be held accountable, punished and rehabilitated for their millions of years of actions.

Yes, you read that correctly, "millions of years". The reptilians have been on Earth for thousands of years trying to destroy humans and feed on our suffering. However, before they came to Earth, they were doing the same thing on many different planets for millions of years. They basically would travel throughout the universe, from planet to planet, lock the planet down in a matrix of fear and suffering and feed on of the beings of that world until they destroyed the entire planet, and then they would move onto the next one.

This goes back all the way to the fallen angels you read about in the Holy Bible. They have turned their back on the light of God, but now they will be paying for their crimes. Balance will be returned to the universe and the light will always win.

Chapter 10

Energy Upgrades, Frequency Changes, Light Codes, Downloads and Channeling

Everyone on Earth has been receiving energy upgrades, experiencing frequency changes, and receiving downloads and light codes for many years since the Ascension process began.

As I mentioned earlier, our DNA is being changed. People who are awake, sensitive, psychic, intuitive, clairvoyant and such can feel, see or hear these experiences when they happen. You know it's happening, or that it *has* happened, because you are tuned into your body, your energy and the universe. We are all like radio receivers and we receive energy signals. We are also like radio stations and broadcast our energy.

Every person on Earth experiences these differently. The people who are still asleep usually have no clue that they are being affected by these energy upgrades. They may complain a little about subtle physical experiences like lack of sleep, headaches, weird body aches, etc., but they have no clue *why* they are having these experiences. Earlier in this book, I also covered Ascension symptoms and these symptoms are a direct result of these energy upgrades, frequency changes, downloads and light codes.

When you receive these upgrades, changes, downloads and codes it is important for you to let go of all fear and just ask your guides and angels to support you through the process. It is also important to keep yourself grounded and centered daily. Spending time in nature every day, or even walking or sitting on grass at least once a day will be helpful for you to integrate all these energetic experiences with fewer negative side effects.

If you are wondering where these upgrades, energy changes, downloads and codes are coming from, these are some of the sources:

- Mother Earth (Gaia) herself
- Our sun
- The Schumann Resonance
- Benevolent star people (ETs) who are here to help us. Some people know them as the Galactic Federation of Light, Pleiadians, Arcturians, Syrians, Lyrians, Nordics, Sphere Being Alliance, Blue Avians and many other races of E.T.s who are here to help us Ascend.
- Higher dimensional beings like Angels, Celestials and other very high dimensional beings
- Christ Consciousness – Yeshua, Buddha and other Ascended Masters
- The Central Sun – The great solar flash that transforms every living thing in the universe will be coming from the central sun
- Your higher Self and oversoul, Your Guides and Your Guardian Angels – mainly give you downloads and assist you in integrating all the codes and energies.

During this Ascension process, some people have received the ability to speak in light language. Light language is a language spoken in higher dimensions. I personally have no idea how to speak in light language, but I have many lightworker friends who do. I also have recorded music that is sung in light language. It is very beautiful and interesting to listen to.

Here is my short list of ways to know that you know you are receiving or have recently received an energy upgrade or vibrational frequency change:

- Feeling much lighter, like a weight has been removed
- Weird or unusual body sensations
- Buzzing feeling all over your body
- Electrical shock sensation

- Out of body sensation
- Feeling spaced out • Foggy brain
- Strange headaches
- Body aches for no reason
- Not wanting to eat any food
- Wanting to eat tons of food like you are starving
- Craving weird foods that you have never craved before
- Need to drink tons of water
- Feeling super hyper for no reason at all
- Tons of energy and feeling like you can clean entire house or dance all night long
- Extreme feelings of love, happiness, excitement, pure joy and bliss for no reason at all
- Unusual negative effects that I listed in the negative ascension symptoms earlier in the book.
- Development of brand new abilities you did not have before, like telepathy or clairaudience.
- Sudden ability to speak in light language or what Christians call "tongues"
- Seeing all sorts of colors around you, including colors you never have seen before on Earth.
- Suddenly being able to see or feel the energy of everything.
- Need to sleep for many hours
- A feeling like you are integrating something but don't know what exactly it is.
- Hearing high pitched sounds in your ears

What is a light Code and how do you know you received one?

A light code is an energy pattern everything in the universe emits.

Within the light codes we find healing energy, Ascension energy, Merkaba/light body upgrades, and important information necessary for you to Ascend. There are also thoughts, words and emotions within the light codes. When all the codes are put together in a pattern it becomes a light language. Light language can also be words that are written or spoken in a sacred universal language.

Everything created emits an energy pattern — your thoughts, feelings and words especially. Words can be translated into symbols and patterns or energy codes, and these become light codes. Many people who are sensitive, intuitive, psychic, clairvoyant, or gifted in other ways are able to see the light language patterns and light codes.

How you know that you are receiving light codes is that when you are meditating you will see strange shapes, symbols, colors and patterns. Sometimes, you will see numbers or strange words in a language you do not recognize. Some of the shapes or symbols you see may be sacred geometry which are very ancient shapes and symbols, used for thousands of years on Earth, by many ancient religions. Seeing these things during meditation is also an indicator that your 3rd eye is opening up and working, and that you are developing special gifts.

When I first started meditating, I began to see weird shapes and colors regularly, and sometimes even people's faces. I would also hear people speaking around me and to me. I occasionally would see a TV-like rectangular screen pop up in front of me with weird binary code or other numbers scrolling across the screen. I recently was in a meditation and had a screen pop up with fluorescent green light language writing. The information on the screen continued for 3 hours.

Yeshua told me that I had had a huge upgrade given to me for my Merkaba (light body). Before I received these light codes and upgrade, I heard a woman's voice say, "*I am joyful to be giving these to you for a second time*". Apparently, these light codes were given to me before I came into this human body so I could lower myself from 12th dimension to 3rd dimension and survive in this human body. I got them again recently to help me upgrade my merkaba for my Ascension.

Typically, when you see light codes, they will appear to you as shapes, patterns or in a series. If you are psychic enough, you will be given names and words for the codes and information you are receiving.

There are many reasons why we receive light codes. Some of the time you are receiving these to help you with Ascension, while at other times you are receiving new abilities, new healing modalities or even a whole new language like light language. You may also be getting healed yourself or receiving abilities for healing others. This is how the inventor of Reiki healing came up with his symbols. When you receive geometric shapes, they can sometimes look like a neon light. At other times they can appear golden or crystalline in nature. I recently had a new spinning 3D geometric shape appear to me that I had never previously seen in my life. The color of it was a light neon green. I have not seen anything on Earth that color before. It was really exciting to see this geometric shape spinning, because it was similar to Ezekiel's wheel that was discussed in the Holy Bible. Sometimes when you receive light codes you will hear a ringing or buzzing, or other weird sound during the transmission. Sometimes I hear music when I receive a light code transmission.

What is a download and how do you know you received one?

A download is different from channeling and you may or may not have control over when one comes to you. Many people confuse those two things. As a psychic and clairvoyant, I receive my information for myself and my clients in many different ways; I receive downloads, I channel information, I hear audible voices, I see visual images, I feel or see energy and I empathically feel info. I also just have a knowing or inner knowledge from my higher self which knows all the answers.

How downloads work is that you receive a piece of information into your mind or energy field, and it comes in suddenly and has a sense of urgency or importance to it.

It could be a creative idea for a new project, new company, new product, new song or important health information. Downloads can manifest like information showing up on a computer screen and they can occur while you are awake, dreaming or meditating. In addition, some people experience a physical feeling while they are receiving a download. It can feel like anticipatory anxiety or it can feel like your head or your entire body are vibrating or pulsating. It can also feel like pure elation, joy, happiness or euphoria. There are also other sensations people feel when a download comes in. Conversely, some people do not have any emotions around a download and only feel peaceful.

That is one of the reasons it is important to improve your mind body connection so you can determine these things. When I receive a download for someone, it is usually important and highly personal information I never knew before. The people on whose behalf I am receiving always confirm it as the truth and are blown away that I knew something about them that they had never told me. For me, downloads are also a sudden experience that seem of arrive from out of nowhere. I have never had control over when and how I get my downloads, but I have friends that have total control over them because they have different psychic gifts than I do.

What is channeling and how do you do it?

Channeling for the first time can be both an exciting and scary experience, especially if you do not know or realize what is happening.

When you channel you are *not* being taken over by an entity unless you have given them permission to come inside of you and take you over. Most people who channel, have information flowing from heaven or higher dimensions through their energy field, etheric field and physical body and then that information manifests in the form of speaking, singing, toning or automatic writing.

My personal experience as a channel was that I started channeling after I gave birth to my kids. Having two vaginal delivery babies gave me a huge kundalini experience and blew open my pineal gland (3rd eye). I developed a multitude of special gifts, one of which was channeling.

How I *knew* I was channeling was that I would start singing a song or humming music I had never heard before. I also would be coaching a client or teaching a class and words started coming out of my mouth that were not from me or my brain. In my case, they were coming from Yeshua, Mary Magdalene and Mother Father God. How I know that is simply because they *told* me. It was as if someone was using my mouth and voice box to speak, but it wasn't me.

I was never scared or worried because every message that has ever come through me in 20 plus years has been pure unconditional love and truth. It has never been dark, negative, critical, derogatory, hateful, judgmental, etc. The information is always accurate, which tends to blow away the people I present it to because there is no way I could have known that information about those people. It has been highly personal and always presented a solution for the people the message came to.

I have also channeled my own messages for myself. I will be praying out loud and all of a sudden a bunch of words come out that represent an important message for me, and it is always helpful. My favorite part of channeling, is when I am teaching a class and have an entire slide show and pages of information ready, and instead of reading what I wrote and practiced, I will start channeling something totally different but much better and much more targeted for the people in the room. I always get people hugging me afterwards which makes me so happy. As long as I am of service to humanity, and the information I am channeling remains positive and beneficial, I will always do this work.

Some people have a great deal of control over their channeling and can do it at the drop of a hat, like Tom Kenyon who channels the Hathors, or Esther Hicks who channels Abraham. I personally do not have control over my channeling. It comes through at the right time and the right place for the right people, but I never know when that is going to be. I simply trust in the process since my sources of channeling are Yeshua, Mary Magdalene and Mother Father God. I have never channeled any other beings.

Please be careful of people who are channeling entities you have never heard of before. The enemy will tell you 99 truths to get across one lie. Also be careful of people claiming to channel archangels. Archangels resonate at such a high frequency and dimension that they are unable to communicate directly with humans. You can send them messages and they will hear those messages and they can send you messages through your guardian angels. Your guardian angels are always the go between for you and the Archangels.

However, you in a human body cannot channel Archangels. Sadly, there are many people who believe they are channeling archangels and some people are lying about it all together because it's a scam. The people who believe they are channeling Archangels are being conned by false light beings, negative E.T.s, demons and archons. It is possible that some of those people may be channeling their own guardian angels and just *think* it's archangels. Please be discerning and protect yourself. I am a human lie detector, so I can always tell phony channels from real channels. In the next chapter I will explain how you can become a channel.

Chapter 11

Communicating and Working with God, Angels, Spirit Guides Ascended Masters and Spirit Animals

Earlier in this book I talked about the way one of your soul purposes is to develop a close relationship and connection with Mother Father God.

In order for you to Ascend, it is very important that you focus on developing this relationship, and that you learn how to communicate with your Creator.

There is a famous quote from the Holy Bible, "*Be still and know 'I AM'*". This quote refers to the fact that you need to quiet your mind in order to hear God and connect with Him/Her. You also need to be able to quiet your mind so you can hear your own inner guidance, your Higher Self, your spirit guides, your guardian angels and Ascended Masters.

Are you able to "*be still and know I AM*"? Are you able to quiet your mind, or do you experience a constant state of "monkey brain" (thoughts going all the time)?

Most humans have monkey brain and consequently find it difficult to quiet their mind.
A large part of the reason can be attributed to this busy world we all live in, full of stress. The majority of humanity is overwhelmed and stressed out, and people do not have peace in their lives.

Does this sound like you? It used to be me, many years ago. Until I was in my early 30's, I could not quiet my mind and I was a "Type A" personality. My life was all go-go-go and could never just sit still and do nothing. I did not know how to quiet my mind and had no clue what present moment awareness was. I was riddled with anxiety and suffered fr(panic attacks. When I was pregnant with my daughter 19(I developed heart problems and tried to keep myself calm but did not have the right tools. After I had her, I started having panic attacks and experienced constant anxiety.

The things that saved my life and healed my anxiety and panic attacks were meditation, mindfulness, pranayama breathing (breathwork), cognitive behavioral therapy, affirmations, mantras, and sound healing. As I practiced these modalities, over time, my mind got quieter and quieter. I was able to be present in the moment, instead of always worrying about the future and dwelling on the past negative events.

If you are wondering how this relates to connecting and communicating with God and the rest of your Holy Spirit team, it has *everything* to do with it. Many years ago, after already having practiced these techniques for at least for 10 years, God spoke to me during meditation and told me that the reason I could hear God and channel Him/Her was because I was able to quiet my mind. God also told me that He/She spoke to every one of His/Her children on Earth, but they were not listening because their minds were too cluttered and busy with other things. God then asked me to teach as many people as possible how to hear Him/Her.

This is a major part of the work I do with my clients. In 2010 I went back to college to become a certified Mindfulness and Meditation Instructor and have been teaching ever since. Although I have had many of my abilities since I was a child, it was after learning to practice mindfulness (present moment awareness) and meditation, that I have been able to develop many more abilities.

Meditation can help to open your 3rd eye and decalcify your pineal gland. Meditation is super beneficial for your brain and body on so many levels, and it can even allow you to release small amounts of a chemical called DMT, which helps you to dissolve your ego. There are altogether 108 types of meditation and they all have many benefits for you, besides helping you to connect with source and develop your psychic and other gifts and abilities.

The first step in being able to communicate with God, higher self, spirit guides, angels and even ghosts and spirits is to learn how to quiet your mind through practicing daily meditation and mindfulness. If you need to learn *how* to do this, please contact me for a group class or private session, but you can also read books and watch videos on the subjects of mindfulness and meditation.

As you practice meditation, each day you will have more and more wonderful experiences and start to hear, feel and see things that you have never experienced before. When this happens, please do not get scared. Simply allow the experience. Always ask (out loud) for protection from your guardian angels and Archangel Michael before you meditate, so that you do not fall victim to psychic attack or communication from any being you do not wish to communicate with.

When humans are born, they usually retain their memories of heaven and who they truly are, at least for the first few years of their lives. During these early years, humans can typically also see their guardian angels and spirit guides as well as elementals like faeries. Many children maintain these abilities until they are four years old. Some remember and see longer. The starseeds — who are highly gifted — will continue doing this the rest of their lives.

The reason you lose this ability by age four is that the more you are brainwashed and indoctrinated into society, the more you forget who you are; the more you forget heaven and lose your ability to see beings. However, you are never too old to remember and when you reach 100% 5th dimension and become fully enlightened, you will most likely remember and see what you have been missing.

There are many ways you can communicate with God and other beings, and there are many ways that they will communicate with you. As you learn how to do this, please make sure to exercise discernment. You will need to learn to distinguish between when the messages are coming from the light and God and when they are coming from dark entities. The messages from God, angels, spirit guides, Ascended Masters, Yeshua and your higher self will always be for your highest good and the good of others. The messages will always be positive. Please keep in mind that Satan, demons and dark entities will tell you 99 truths to get one lie across, so you must proceed with caution.

The messages over time should always be good when they are coming from the light. Here are some typical methods of spiritual communication:

The best way to speak to and connect with Mother Father God:

- Prayer, directly yourself or intercessory prayer
- Meditation – the more you meditate the more you will be able to receive messages
- Have a conversation out loud with God. God is your heavenly parent so you can speak like you would with your Earth parents.
- Singing (praise and worship music)
- Chanting "OM" – the primordial sound of the universe that all creation came from. You can also chant the word "Shalom" which means peace in Hebrew language and also contains the word "OM" within it.
- Other types of chanting – (In English, Latin, Sanskrit or other languages) Used in all ancient religions as well as by monks and nuns

Ways Mother-Father God communicates with you:

- Answering prayers and requests – Example: you receive a job, receiving healing or receiving money you need, etc.
- Hearing God's audible voice
- Receiving downloads
- Channeling God
- Automatic writing – You need a paper and pen or pencil for this
- Music — you hear a song that conveys a message or you hear music with your psychic hearing (clairaudience). Some people hear heavenly music or a heavenly choir
- Through other people – God often uses other people to give you messages. This is something I have experienced my entire life
- Nature – God always communicates through nature
- Animals and pets
- Signs, symbols and numbers that have meaning to you
- Visions while you are awake
- Dreams while you are asleep – In the Bible there are stories of God communicating with people through their dreams
- Near Death Experience
- Miracles
- Intuitive feelings and sensations
- Muscle testing – You can ask God "Yes" and "No" questions and use muscle testing to establish an answer

The best way to communicate with your guardian angels is by simply speaking to them out loud. They are not allowed to read your mind because of the laws of the universe concerning privacy and free will. They are not supposed to interfere with your life unless you ask them. The reason they are able to help you when you are in trouble, even if you don't speak out loud to them, is that they can see with their eyes and hear with their ears what is happening to you in the present moment, as well as in the past and the future.

Angels exist in the past, present and future and in all timelines simultaneously, since there is no time in their dimension. They can see if you are about to be in an accident and protect you. But when you want their immediate help you must open your mouth and ask them out loud.

Gratitude matters! Please remember to thank your angels regularly and show them gratitude, because they work hard to keep you safe every day and make sure that you finish your life according to your plan and God's plan for you.

If you want to speak to Archangels, you just address them out loud directly and they will hear you, or your guardian angels will deliver the messages for you. For example, if you want Archangel Michael or Raphael's help, you simply say out loud *"I call in Archangel Michael and Archangel Raphael and ask you to help me"*.

They will hear you and come to assist. If for some reason they are unavailable, your guardian angels will work as intermediaries. Archangels are not able to speak to you directly, channel through you or give you signs because they reside in such a high dimension that you will not be able to hear them. However, your guardian angels always act as intermediaries and can relay the messages to you.

Many people believe they are channeling or hearing archangels, but they are actually hearing and getting those messages from their guardian angels, guides or other beings who are messengers or intermediaries for the higher dimensional Archangels. Some people are tricked by false light beings into thinking they are hearing Archangels when they are actually hearing malevolent E.T.s, archons or demonic entities so be very careful when exploring this area.

If you want to know the name of your angels, just ask them out loud and wait to receive an answer.

Some of the many methods that your guardian angels communicate with you:

- Visions and dreams – Some of my guardian angels have introduced themselves to me in my dreams. I have also seen them in visions.
- Hearing their audible voice (clairaudience)
- Sacred geometry, shapes and symbols
- Numbers – You may see a pattern of numbers showing up in your daily life for example 111, 1111, 1212, 222, 333, 444, 555, 666, 777, 888 and 999. You may also see series of numbers like 123. I have even received numbers like 909, 808, 911 and 411. There are many websites on the Internet that offer extensive information on angel numbers.
- Angel oracle cards or Tarot cards – You can ask your angels a question and get an answer with these cards
- Automatic writing – You need a paper and pen or pencil for this
- Music — you hear a song that gives you a message or you hear music with your psychic hearing (clairaudience). Some people hear heavenly music or a heavenly choir.
- Through intuitive feelings and sensations
- Through other people – Sometimes angels give us messages through other people, the same way God does.
- Animals and pets
- Near Death Experience – Many people meet their guardian angels when they have a near death experience.

- Synchronicities – Example: You run into people you haven't seen in a while and you were thinking about them immediately before you ran into them.

- Physical touch – Angels can touch you on your head, shoulder, hand, arm, back, leg or foot to let you know they are there for you. Some people even set up a system of "Yes and no" answers to questions by having their angels touch them on the left hand or right hand or left shoulder or right shoulder.

- They can physically manifest and appear in front of you. I have recently seen several photos and videos that various people have taken of angels. They were beautiful and made entirely of bright white light. Some were white with other rainbow colors.

Your spirit guides are beings you pick to assist you before you incarnate into a human or other body on Earth and other planets. They help you write up your life plan contract and they assist and guide you while you are on Earth and on other planets.

You can talk to them anytime and ask them questions or to assist you, but you need to speak to them out loud. Just like your angels have rules, your guides have the same rules to not interfere in your life unless necessary and they cannot read your mind. You need to use your voice to ask them for help.

Just like communicating with God and angels, asking your spirit guides questions, and then meditating and quieting your mind so you can hear their guidance, is the best way to work with them. If you want to know who your guides are, just ask them out loud to reveal their names to you.

Some of the methods your Spirit Guides use to communicate with you:

- You may hear their audible voice
- Visions and dreams
- Through sacred geometry, shapes and symbols
- Downloads
- Channeled messages
- Automatic writing – You need a paper and pen or pencil for this
- Near Death Experience – Many people meet their spirit guide team when they have a near death experience.

Ascended Masters and other Spiritual high dimensional beings:

Yeshua (the Christ), Mary Magdalene, Mother Mary, Buddha, Sananda, Maitreya, White Buffalo Calf Woman, Quan Yin, St. Germain, and many others are Ascended Masters.

These are beings who are of the highest dimensions who have achieved total enlightenment. They have come to Earth during the history of this planet to teach and help humanity with our Ascension, enlightenment, and teach us how to have a relationship with Mother Father God. Some of these beings are known as Christed beings and make up what is called Christ Consciousness, which is the highest achievement a dimensional being can make.

Angels cannot be part of Christ consciousness. However, angels can incarnate into human or other bodies and eventually become Ascended Masters before they return to the angelic realm. There are also some beings who are Ascended Masters but not part of
Christ Consciousness. Many of the ancient Gods and Goddess like Lakshmi, Vishnu, Durga, Kali, Isis, Zeus, Apollo, Athena, etc. are actually very powerful ancient extraterrestrials who came to Earth thousands and years ago. Humans thought they were God and called them Gods and Goddesses.

The hierarchy of the high spiritual realm looks like this:

Mother Father God Source

Archangels

Angels – (Includes different levels of angelic beings)

Christ Consciousness – Yeshua and team

Ancient Gods/Goddesses (Powerful high-dimensional E.T.s)

Ascended Masters

The best way to communicate with the Ascended Masters, Christed beings and Ancient Gods and Goddesses is by asking them out loud for help and then quieting your mind for the answers.

The only beings — besides Mother/Father God — who are allowed to read your thoughts and silent prayers are Yeshua, Mother Mary, Buddha and the members of Christ Consciousness. Regular Ascended Masters who are not part of Christ Consciousness cannot read your thoughts. There are negative E.T.s that may try to read your thoughts, and some humans who have telepathic abilities might read your thoughts but if they do that without your free will consent, they are breaking universal laws and they will have to be held accountable for that.

Some of the methods Yeshua and other members of Christ Consciousness, as well as Ascended Masters and the high dimensional E.T.s (Ancient Gods), use to communicate with you are:

- Answering prayers and requests
- Hearing their audible voice
- Receiving downloads
- Channeling
- Automatic writing
- Music
- Through other people
- Animals and pets
- Signs, symbols and numbers that have meaning to you
- Visions while you are awake
- Dreams while you are asleep
- Near Death Experiences
- Miracles
- Intuitive feelings and sensations
- Muscle testing for yes or no answers
- Sacred geometry and shapes
- Physical touch
- They can physically manifest and appear in front of you

Spirit Animals (Totems):

In many ancient cultures, especially indigenous native cultures of North America, South America, Pacific Islands, Australia and New Zealand there is a belief that people can have animal spirit guides or protectors. These can also include birds, water-based creatures and insects.

Some people even have mythological spirit animals like a dragon or Yeti. A number of the creatures people believe are myths, are actually interdimensional creatures and are very real.

My personal spirit animals are White Wolf, Eagle, Hawk, and Dragonfly. Some of these animals will show up during the day and visit you to bring you a message or get your attention. Some of them will appear in your meditations, your dreams at night or in visions during the day. Sometimes these spirit animals will physically show up in your home, office, garden, in front of your car, while you're on a walk and in other places.

You must be open to their energy and paying attention to your surroundings. Being present in the moment is a key element for seeing them during the day.

There are many books that can help you interpret messages when spirit animals pay you a visit. There are also websites where you can find a wealth of information on spirit animal messages.

Spirit animals will usually communicate with you just by showing up at exactly the right time and place, but they can also send you telepathic messages. When you are intuitive or clairvoyant you can decipher their messages more easily.

Do you know which animals are your spirit totems or guides? If not, then one way to figure out which ones are yours, is to consider whether you are obsessed with, or highly attracted to, a specific animal. Another approach is to consider whether you have visions of a specific animal, bird or insect or see the same one in your dreams repeatedly. If there is a specific animal that shows up in front of you regularly, that is another way. For example, if you always have an Eagle nesting in your yard or you constantly have butterflies landing on you, that would be an indication that maybe they are a spirit animal.

When you dream or meditate you may see other animals, birds and insects appear that are different from your spirit guide animal. That is when it becomes important to research their meaning in a book or website, unless you have intuitive abilities and can use your own gifts to arrive at an answer.

If you don't feel attracted to a specific animal and have no experience seeing them in dreams or visions, it may mean that you don't have an animal spirit guide. There is nothing wrong with this because not all people have them.

If you don't have a spirit animal and you want one, you can ask your guides and angels if one can be sent to you. You have free will to choose who is guiding you in the first place.

Animals vibrate at a very high frequency and are extremely helpful for your Ascension. Their energy is pure love without judgement, hate or any of the negative ego properties that humans possess, so they can help you transmute energies in a loving way. Pets are actually some of the best animals to help you through your Ascension process. They offer us their unconditional love, compassion and healing. Pets raise your vibration purely as a result of you spending time with them and showing them love.

Ghosts and Spirits:

Because the veil is getting thinner as we Ascend, you may have had one or more experiences with the ghosts or spirits of passed away family and friends. I have had many such experiences since I was a child.

I am not going to cover communication with ghosts and spirits in this book because it will not help you with your Ascension and my mediumship skills are limited. If you want to know how to be a medium and communicate with ghosts and spirits of deceased loved ones, I have many resources I can send you to for that information and training. Please contact me through my website.

Extraterrestrials:

You can contact and be contacted by Star People (Extraterrestrials), or you can be contacted by the beings living in cities in the inner Earth, however I am not going to cover that in this book, since I am only focused on spiritual and esoteric concepts of Earth and our Ascension.

There are literally hundreds of books about E.T. contact and many people you can follow and watch videos from like David Wilcock, Corey Good, Magenta Pixie and Elizabeth April. These are just a few of the many people who have been in contact with the Galactic Federation and other benevolent extraterrestrials who are here to help us with our Ascension.

Ancient Aliens is one of my favorite shows that exposes the history of E.T.s visiting Earth. I do not work with those beings, so I am not a good authority on them. However, I *will* tell you that some of the best places in the USA to see U.F.O.s include Arizona (especially Sedona), Nevada (Henderson), New Mexico, Washington State, Oregon, Mount Shasta, the mountains of North Carolina, the mountains of Arkansas, Appalacian mountains, Hawaii, Alaska, ECETI ranch and the Skinwalker Ranch. Other great places to have a close encounter outside the U.S. are Peru, certain locations in Central and South America, the South Pacific, and Australia.

Prayer, intention and manifesting:

Humans have always been able to manifest and co-create their reality with God. However, since we started going through this Ascension process, our ability to instantly manifest is becoming stronger. This means that whatever you believe, think about, speak about and focus on, will become your reality. You will attract more of whatever your focus is directed at. If you are trapped in a place of fear, you will attract negative things into your life, leading to mental and physical illness.

From this point forward, please make sure that all your thoughts, words and beliefs are positive. Make sure that when you pray you are being very specific about your intentions. Always be as specific as possible when you ask your guides, angels, God, and Ascended Masters for help. Every time you pray, be as specific and detailed as possible.

When I pray to God, I like to refer to Him/Her as "Mother Father God of Love" or "Divine Mother Father God Creator of my soul". I do this to make sure I am praying to the right creative source. This is important because throughout history there have been *many* Gods and Goddesses.

When you pray to God, it doesn't matter who you pray to or what you call them. So, don't worry about praying the way that I do. God has gone by hundreds of names throughout the history of the world. Everyone prays to a different God and that is okay.

What is important is the *intention and focus* of your prayer. Everything is energy, frequency and vibration, including prayer. Prayer can be a request, question, intention, want, need and wish. Yeshua said, *"ask and you shall receive"* and "knock and a door shall be opened."

So when you are praying, you are doing just that, but you also need faith and the belief that your prayers will be answered. If you don't ask and then believe, you may not receive. Your belief is one of the most powerful vibrations you possess. Also, when you pray, the universe and God will give you exactly what you ask for, based on *how* you asked for it. As a consequence, you have to be really careful about what you ask for, wish for and say. Your speech is more powerful than your thoughts so if you speak a prayer verbally you really need to be careful.

An illustration of being careful with prayer, could be that you pray for "a bunch of money," as a result of which you could get into a car accident, get injured badly and as a result of a law suit against a negligent driver you get "a bunch of money," while being confined to a wheelchair.

You need to be specific with your prayers and intentions, so you get exactly what it is that you want. Example: *"Divine source I need $20,000 to pay off my bills and I would love to receive it through a business venture, job or lottery winnings and wish to receive it in a way that is for my highest good and best interest."*

When you want to ask specific questions of God, angels, guides, etc., the best thing you can do is ask the question, keep a paper and pen next to you and sit in a meditation for a while to listen for the answer. You can practice this method of question and answer daily so that you become adept at receiving messages.

Chapter 12

The Darkness Within – Your Shadow Self and Dark Night of the Soul

Everyone on the spiritual journey goes through at least one or more dark nights of the soul. Every human has a shadow side that creates these events that happen in our lives. Until you reach total enlightenment, you will always have a shadow side that rears its ugly head and causes negative issues in your life. Part of your Ascension process is learning how to embrace and heal your shadow self. You cannot Ascend without working on your shadow self.

In this chapter we will cover what the shadow self and dark night of the soul are by definition, and then we will examine methods you can use to heal.

What is a shadow self?

According to Wikipedia psychology:

> "In Jungian psychology, the "shadow", "id", or "shadow aspect/archetype" may refer to (1) an unconscious aspect of the personality which the conscious ego does not identify in itself, or (2) the entirety of the unconscious, i.e., everything of which a person is not fully conscious. In short, the shadow is the unknown."

When a human is born, they are a pure innocent blank canvas, and as they grow older, they learn ideas, beliefs, emotions, behaviors, and feelings from the world around them, some of which may not be positive or good.

They learn these things from parents and family, neighbors, friends, teachers, advertising, television, movies, magazines, their community, and society in general. Over time, you learn what is "good" and what is considered "evil" and you learn to repress everything that is considered negative, wrong or evil into your subconscious and unconscious mind, where they become part of you.

On the whole, you have no idea that these negative or evil things exist within you because you have buried them that deeply into your subconscious and unconscious mind. You repress these things that you have learned, and they gradually become your shadow self. Very likely, you'll go through your entire life having no idea that these things live inside of your brain and effect you on a mental, emotional, energetic and physical level.

These negative things buried inside you are hiding in the background and are creating mental and physical illnesses. Many of the illnesses you experience in your life are caused by things you have repressed that now make up your shadow self. These buried feelings can lead to many psychological symptoms in the form of neuroses and psychoses, depression, anxiety, paranoia, mood swings, and a myriad of other mental health problems.

Every human on Earth has a shadow self or shadow side; even the most pure and noble truthful beings have a shadow side. You cannot blame anyone for this because they are a creation of society and their upbringing. People who seem truly evil are fully consumed by their shadow side.

The only way to heal the shadow side is by confronting it and doing the work. Healing your shadow side is not something that you can accomplish overnight. For some people it can take months, years or even a lifetime. The important thing in the present moment is that you need to work on healing your shadow side and heal as much of it as you can so you can raise your vibration and make it through the Ascension process with your sanity and your health intact.

> *"The unconscious is not just evil by nature, it is also the source of the highest good: not only dark but also light, not only bestial, semi-human, and demonic but superhuman, spiritual, and, in the classical sense of the word, "divine."* – Carl Jung

How to heal your shadow self:

1. Find a good spiritual psychology practitioner who can help you work with your shadow side, because even though you can do some of this work by yourself, you need to have consistent support to be successful. Much of the shadow work I have done on myself over the years, has been with the help of my guides and angels, because I am able to hear and see them with my 3rd eye. However, I have also needed human expert support and have had experienced spiritual and psychological counselors help me and support me over the years. If you need a recommendation for an expert who specializes in shadow work, please contact me through my website for recommendations.

2. Get rid of victim mentality. Instead of feeling sorry for yourself and dwelling on all the negative things from your past that you have said, done or learned, learn to hold yourself accountable for them without feeling sorry for yourself. The fact is that all humans have problems and issues. No human is perfect. It's important for you to accept the fact that you are in a human body with a human brain and that you are not broken or flawed. Accept that you have made mistakes and bad choices in the past and that the people who have influenced your mind and life also have made

mistakes and bad choices. When you are able to acknowledge and accept that you *do* have a shadow side, and that you are willing to heal it, then you have won most of the battle.

3. Practice self-love and self-worth – You are loved, and you are worthy, but you must believe that yourself. If you do not love yourself or believe that God loves you, and you do not feel worthy, then you cannot heal yourself. Love is the most powerful healer and so is belief. You have an unconditionally loving creator; you are worthy of good things. The Catholic Church and other religions have taught you lies to control you, to separate you from God with duality and get you to pay them for forgiveness. That is a lie because in God's loving eyes you are always worthy. Believe that your life can — and will — get better and that you are worthy of receiving miracles.

4. Go into this work with strength and bravery, knowing that you are going to see, hear and learn things about yourself that you do not like and that will upset you. Things that you never would have imagined will be coming up to the surface for healing. You are going to feel uncomfortable and maybe even disgusted or sick when certain things come up for you to face, but keep in mind that this a good thing because without that, you cannot heal your shadow. During this Ascension and with every new wave of energy hitting the Earth, people are experiencing all their shadow stuff rise up to the surface for release and healing. It may seem ugly, but you are fully able to change yourself for the better, as well as heal and raise your vibration by doing this important work.

5. The next step in the process of healing your shadow is for you to practice mindfulness daily and pay

attention to all your thoughts, feelings and emotions as they arise.

I have been teaching Mindfulness (present moment awareness) to my clients since 2011. When you practice mindfulness, you watch your thoughts, feelings and emotions like a lab experiment and determine whether they are good, bad or neutral. You can go deep into examining everything that comes up for you during your day and notice how your body is affected. As the thoughts, feelings and emotions come up you can analyze, categorize and determine whether they are beneficial or harmful so that you can clear and heal things as needed.

The best way to deal with this is to ask yourself questions like, *"What am I feeling? Is this good or bad? Is this beneficial for me? Why am I thinking or feeling this?"* Listen intuitively for the answers to your questions. You may or may not get any. If you do not get answers that's okay, don't beat yourself up. With time, practice and work the process will get easier and all will be revealed. You need to believe and have faith that this process will work out for you. The practice of mindfulness itself is healing, even when you are not using it to do shadow work.

It is very beneficial to be mindful every day of your life. As you explore your thoughts, feelings and emotions, do not stuff them or run away from them if you don't like them, because that will only create a bigger shadow and cause mental and physical illness. Instead, face everything head-on and look at it with strength and maturity. Healing comes when you step into your own power.

6. You will identify your shadow — or parts of your shadow — by noticing the recurring patterns of your

feelings, thoughts and emotions, after you have practiced mindfulness for a while. There are many common themes of false beliefs that come to the surface for people including:

- I am not worthy
- I am not good enough
- I am not loved
- I am flawed
- I am stupid
- I am a sinner
- I am always sick
- I am a failure
- I am not important
- I am never listened to
- I am never successful
- I can't make money
- I am broken
- I will never find love

There are literally *hundreds* of false beliefs people have in their subconscious and conscious mind, but these are some of the biggest. As you notice your negative emotions, always accept the fact that it is human and perfectly fine to have them. You are not bad, broken or a failure for having negative emotions.

7. Be in a state of constant gratitude for the healing work you are doing for yourself. You are giving yourself the best gift ever by working on your shadow. Also be super compassionate and loving with yourself as you go through this healing process. As old traumas are brought up to the surface for release, it may be difficult, so maintain patience and compassion for yourself.

8. Never blame other people for your shadow side. Everything that makes up you and who you are today

was all agreed upon by you before you came here. Any person who caused trauma in your life or impacted you in a negative way was playing a part in your learning journey.

If they were doing something evil or harmful to humans like pedophilia, torture, rape, abuse, etc. they will be held accountable for their crimes and will receive a punishment. However, they were still playing a role in the development of who you are and where you are going in your journey.

My own example of this is that I had to go through a lot of childhood trauma healing from having a mother who was psychologically abusive and sometimes physically abusive. I did tons of inner child work, and there was a time when I would blame my mother for all my problems. As I healed myself, I learned that what happened to me was not her fault, because we agreed upon our relationship before we came here. I chose her to be my mother for certain learning reasons.

I have learned so much from the experience and grown as a person and a soul. I am who I am today as a spiritual teacher because of my mother and the things I learned from that relationship. Now I am grateful for the experience and have forgiven her, even though it was unpleasant. I had to learn about her background and why she made the wrong choices she did. In her case, her childhood experience was traumatic and negative, and she never healed it. As a result she took her trauma out on me.

As you do this work, it is important to understand why the people who hurt you acted the way they did. It may be very hard to accept what they did, but you have to forgive everyone who has ever hurt you in order to heal yourself mentally, emotionally, physically and energetically, and in order to Ascend with a high vibration.

9. Learn how to identify the shadow or dark emotions that you have within you and do not feel guilty or ashamed of what you find within yourself. These emotions come from the negative and unhealthy part of the ego. Some of the more common negative emotions and feelings many people have stored within their shadow side include shame, blame, guilt, unforgiveness, anger, hate, fear, loathing, jealousy, greed, malice, superiority, know-it-all, competition, grief, sadness, despair, envy, anxiety, panic, depression, regret, sorrow, misery, hostility, rage, cynicism, sarcasm, insecurity, embarrassment, worry, resentment, heartache, regret, misery, pain, insecurity, betrayal, suffering and more.

10. Inner child work – Every person on the Earth has had one or more traumatic things happen while they were a baby or child. It could just be the traumatic way they entered the world, or it could be events like emotional or physical abuse, rape, molestation, war, serious illness, losing parents, serious accidents and injuries, betrayal, being bullied, hate crimes, watching someone else be harmed or killed, starvation, abandonment, suffering, lack of love, pain, and various other types of trauma.

    In order to heal your shadow side and Ascend, it is important for you to do healing work with your inner child. That is the part of you that was wounded or traumatized when you were young and has been repressed and hiding within your subconscious and unconscious mind, all of these years.

If you do not heal your inner child wounds and trauma it can negatively impact all of your relationships, your ability to love and be loved, your ability to make money, your ability to be mentally and physically healthy, your career or business, and it will lower your vibration and either slow down your Ascension or prevent you from Ascending altogether.

My personal experience involved finding out that I had a few health problems that wouldn't heal no matter what I tried, until I healed my inner child. Only then was I able to heal the health issues related to the inner child wounds. I have a few people I work with on inner child issues and would be happy to refer you if you need someone to help you. Just contact me through my website for the referral.

11. Meditate at least once a day and ask Mother/Father God, your guides and angels, and anyone else you would like to assist you in bringing to the surface any shadow emotions, traumas, wounds or experiences that need to be cleared and healed.

12. Keep a journal while you are doing your shadow work. You will need to take notes every time anything comes up that is helpful to your healing.

13. Practice Ho'oponopono, the ancient Hawaiian forgiveness prayer. Holding onto unforgiveness will make you sick and blocks your heart chakra. Make a list of every person who has hurt you since you were young. Imagine standing in front of each one of them and forgiving them with this prayer and then imagine the cord connecting you and the person being cut and the person fading away into the clouds. You can also ask Archangel Michael to help you cut cords tying you to people in your past who have hurt you. Archangel

Michael is really good at using his sword to cut cords. The Ho'oponopono prayer is:

"I am sorry
Please forgive me
I love you
Thank you"

14. Pay attention to your dreams – A lot of shadow stuff can show up in your dreams. The things that happen in your dreams are often symbolic of things going on in your conscious and subconscious mind. Your dreams are where your brain works out all your problems in life, and your deepest thoughts and emotions will show up in your dreams.

    Keep a note pad and paper by the side of your bed and write down whatever you can remember from your dreams. You can look up the information in books or online or you can work with a Jungian therapist to find out what your dreams mean. This will help you escalate your shadow side healing work.

What is a Dark Night of the Soul?

Almost every human will go through one or more "dark nights of the soul" in their lifetime.

I have been through this event many times in my life and emerged from each a smarter, wiser and stronger person. That old phrase, "What doesn't kill you makes you stronger", is 100% true!

The way I like to describe the dark night of the soul is when you go through one or more terrible things in your life and you hit rock bottom or you get to a point where you are depressed, lose faith and hope, run out of patience, become fully disgusted, unhappy and miserable, and you feel like your life totally sucks. It's that moment in time when you feel deep depression, psychosis, nervous breakdown, and have feelings of being totally lost and hopeless.

This event can go on for days, weeks or even months before you have a healing breakthrough and snap out of it. Although you may think that going through a dark night of the soul experience is horrible, it is actually a good thing, because it is offering you a period of spiritual learning and growth. After you make it out on the other end, you will have a closer relationship with God.

As a spiritual being you cannot move forward, learn or grow without these experiences in life. During a dark night of the soul you can experience an ego death. The whole experience is a sort of death and rebirth. The "*you*" who enters the experience is different from the "you" that comes out the other end. It is similar to the Hero's Journey.

While every human being will experience pain and hardship, not everyone will experience the dark night of the soul. This experience represents a major transformation and alteration of everything you thought you knew. You may even feel like you are dying, but the only thing dying is your ego. When you go through these experiences, it forces you to ask questions you never asked before or even thought of asking, such as "What is my purpose? Why am I here? Does God hear me or care about me? Does God really exist? Where am I going with my life? Why have I made so many mistakes?" along with lots of other questions.

How to Overcome and Recover From the Dark Night of the Soul

Spending some time alone is always helpful when you go through this experience. However, you also need support from other people, especially when you feel like you are losing your mind.

There is a difference between someone with serious clinical depression and mental illness and someone going through a dark night of the soul. The prior needs medication and lots of counseling. When you go through a dark night of the soul you do not need drugs and you do not necessarily need counseling, however counseling is definitely helpful to get through this experience.

If you choose counseling, you need to make sure you are working with a counselor who is spiritually based since this is really a very spiritual experience. A regular psychotherapist who does not have spiritual beliefs or a spiritual background will not be beneficial.

Everyone has bad things happen in their lifetime, negative experiences and difficult situations, but those are completely different from a dark night of the soul experience. You will know it when you have it because it will take to a place you have never been where you start questioning everything including you own existence. If you believe you are having a dark night of the soul experience, just allow it to fully envelop you. Submerge yourself into it and allow everything to come up to the surface for healing. Do not try to fight it or stop it, instead, allow yourself to go through this experience and trust that you will be okay and protected. Be patient with yourself; trust and understand that your soul knows exactly how long this process will take place and why you are going through it.

Here are some other recommendations for getting through this process:

1. Fully submerge yourself into the experience.

2. Listen to your body and take really good care of it with healthy diet, plenty of sleep and naps when necessary, exercise and move your body daily.

3. Practice Mindfulness to deal with all the emotions that are coming up. I mentioned this previously in this book.

4. Spend time every day in meditation. Start out with five minutes a day and work your way up to 20 minutes to an hour.

5. Do breathing exercises daily. Learn how to practice pranayama breathing or just spend at least a few minutes or more each day focusing on your breath in and out through your nose.

6. Drink lots of purified mineral water every day.

7. Listen to high vibrational music, especially music that is 528 HZ love frequency. It will help you to heal through your experience and is great for emotional and energetic clearing.

8. Spend time with your friends and stay connected to people. Total isolation is not beneficial. Isolating yourself for small amounts of time is okay but we all need each other to survive on Earth. For people who suffer from depression, it is very difficult to feel isolated or disconnected from the world and from other people, so connecting with friends helps you break out of the depressive cycle.

9. Do things that make you feel happiness and joy – working in the garden, watching comedy movies, listening to beautiful music, playing games, having sex, eating yummy food, etc.

10. Spend time with pets since they have a healing effect on humans.

11. Work with a spiritual counselor.

12. Spend time in nature and connect with our Mother Gaia.

13. Ground yourself daily by walking barefoot or sitting on the grass or a beach.

14. Spend time reading spiritual books, especially those that are uplifting and bring you peace.

15. Keep a journal and write in it every day.

16. Daily prayer and connecting with God is most important, since one of the major reasons you go through a dark night of the soul event is to allow you to strengthen your spiritual relationship with God.

17. Be loving and compassionate with yourself. You are not broken, flawed or a failure; instead you are going through an incredible growth period. Look at this experience as a positive one.

18. Use different energy healing modalities to clear away negative energies and heal your chakras.

19. Work with crystals. There are many crystals good for grounding and clearing energy as well as for emotional healing and giving you peaceful feelings. My favorite crystal to work with when I feel anxious or depressed — or I'm going through the dark night of the soul — is Amethyst. It is a very soothing stone that works with your 3rd eye and crown chakra and transmutes negative energies.

20. Do not watch or listen to the news, with exception of checking the weather. Do not watch any violent T.V. shows or movies and do not read negative posts or stories on social media. The reason being that you are *already* going through depressing or difficult emotions and you need to focus on working through them and raising your vibration. When you focus on negative things like the news,
violent shows and negative posts, it will drag you down to an even darker more depressing place than you are already experiencing while going through your dark night of the soul event. You need to keep your focus on things of beauty and high vibration to help you get through this period on your journey.

Chapter 13

Service to Self vs. Service to Others

In order to Ascend with the planet and survive the solar flash that is prophesied to hit the Earth by 2030, you need to be 60% or more "love based" and "service to others or service to Earth based."

If you have never heard the term "service to others," it basically means you are a kind, loving compassionate human who does nice deeds for other people. When you are in service to the planet or in service to others, you embrace that you are connected to every living person and every living creature on the planet.

You may feel that you are equal to everyone on Earth and that you are not more important or more special than other humans. You care about other people and are conscious of what is going on with other people. You take care of people and their needs, maybe putting others like your family members before yourself. You are helpful to other people and treat other humans with compassion, kindness, and respect. You do things to help whenever you are able. You may work with or live with pets or animals and you love and respect all living creatures.

There are many people on this Earth who unfortunately live in a perpetual state of service to *self*. To stay in a high vibration and Ascend you need to be all or mostly "service to others". If you are 20% or more "service to self" you risk creating bad karma in this lifetime or your next. You will slow down or prevent your Ascension and you will be stuck in a low vibration.

As I mentioned above, there are many people on Earth who unfortunately live their lives practicing "service to self." They rarely, if ever, help other people. These same people spend their lives using things and using people to get what they want, without a second thought to the consequences of their actions. They constantly seek out ways to make more money, buy more material possessions, get promoted as much as possible, become wealthy and famous, have lots of meaningless sexual affairs and constantly focus on self-gratification.

They will do just about anything to protect themselves even if it hurts others. These are the same people who step on people's heads to climb to the top. They also backstab people to get what they want. They are very jealous, possessive, and selfish as friends and lovers, so they typically fail spectacularly at relationships. They may be totally untrustworthy and tell lies. They are probably narcissists.

Some of them may have the outward *appearance* of a happy life and "having it all" but they are never really happy. Most are totally empty inside. People who know these types of people will sometimes say that they are missing their soul. Unfortunately for them, living a life centered on "service-to-self" causes a low vibration, prolongs and prevents Ascension and creates bad karma that will keep the self-serving individual stuck on the rat wheel of Samsara.

They will reincarnate many lifetimes until they figure out that, in order to Ascend, there needs to be a healthy balance between service to self and service to others. If you want to maintain a high vibration and

Ascend, you need to be mostly "service to others" and if possible 100% "service to others". You should be in a constant state of love, kindness, and compassion.

The people who are primarily "service to self" are blocked in their heart chakras and live in a state of FEAR instead of LOVE. People who are LOVE based understand the importance of service to others.

There are many reasons why people live their lives in the "service to self" cycle. Some of them experienced trauma during childhood, some have psychological problems, some have extremely low self-esteem, some never received love, some are just playing out a role (like a Shakespeare play) to serve a spiritual purpose on Earth, some are being controlled by dark demonic entities, some lack intelligence and some of them are just very bad people.

If you know people like this, you need to protect your energy from them and forgive them for not being on the same path as you are. Yeshua said "*Forgive them Father they know not what they do.*" Think of these people as kindergarten souls who have a long road to get to the same level of education you are currently at. Look at it as similar to being on the playground with preschoolers when you are in college. If the preschoolers throw sand at you or a toy at your head, you forgive them for being young, un-educated and not knowing better. It is the same with "service to self" people. They really don't know any better, and they have a very long journey ahead of them. Some of these people may have millions of years of lifetimes before they catch up to the level you are at right now.

If you are reading this book, then most likely you are like myself and live your life mostly or all the way in "service to others".

"Service to self" vs. "Service to others" is a spiritual state of mind, belief system and choices, and it is a completely different thing from "giving and receiving". If you are someone like myself who gives too much to others and doesn't receive as much, you can literally make yourself sick, because people are draining your energy all the time and you are not replenishing it.

This is something I have struggled with for many years because I love helping people so much and I am always kind to everyone. My mother taught me to treat others as I wanted to be treated, and I have probably practiced that a little too well!

I am still working on my *receiving*. When it comes to giving and receiving it should be balanced 50/50 as much as possible. Check in with your higher self or your spirit guides and ask yourself how much you are giving, versus how much you are receiving. If you are not receiving in a balanced way, or 50% of the time, then you need to find out why you are not receiving and fix it.

When we say receiving, we are talking about receiving health or healing, abundance, respect, friendship, financial prosperity, jobs, promotions, support, assistance, friends, love, happiness, and other positive things that you deserve. Many people refer to the receiving end as manifestation. If you are not receiving enough then you are blocked. Some of the many reasons you are not receiving enough include:

- You don't feel worthy or deserving of receiving.
- Past life-time oaths, contracts, karma and trauma. You could have been a nun or priest in a past life and took an oath of poverty.

160

- Current lifetime subconscious and conscious beliefs. Conscious beliefs are ones that you know at the top of your mind, for example, "I am not worthy. Nobody loves me. I am not smart enough. I am not important, and I don't matter. I will never be successful". These conscious beliefs came from teachings or events from your childhood. Your family, neighbors, teachers, society, and the media all contributed to both your conscious and your subconscious beliefs.

  Subconscious beliefs are beliefs that you don't know or realize you have and they have gone into the annals of your mind and into your DNA because of past lifetime experiences, all your current life experiences, things people have said to you since birth, society and many other causes. These subconscious beliefs stay in you until you clear them out.
- Psychic attack by other humans, demonic entities, negative E.T.s, witchcraft, voodoo.

If you are someone who gives too much and you need to start receiving more good stuff, then I recommend finding a shaman, spiritual counselor, lightworker or healer who can work with you to uncover the blocks and clear and heal them.
You are worthy, you are loved, and you deserve to always receive an abundance of all things that are good!

I offer this service to my clients, and you can contact me through my website www.spiritualgrowthjourneys.com . If I am unable to assist you, I can refer you to someone who I believe is good at clearing out blocks to receiving and abundance. I have a list of many people I have known for a long time and trust.

Chapter 14

Happiness: Your True Purpose

"The purpose of our lives is to be happy"

His holiness the Dalai Lama

One of the main purposes of your soul is to just be happy. The other primary purpose is love but when you love and are loved then you are also happy. Achieving happiness is part of your Ascension plan, but being happy also raises your vibration, to assist with this process on Earth.

One of my favorite quotes ever written is attributed to President Abraham Lincoln:

"Most people are as happy as they make up their minds to be"

Creating happiness is very important in maintaining a high vibration for your Ascension. Happiness is also a thing that our loving Creator always wants for us. Unfortunately, the reality is that most people *choose* to be unhappy and/or don't understand that it is 100% up to them to create their own happiness.

That's right, it's not the job of your spouse, girlfriend, jewelry, Porsche, a mansion, etc. to make you happy. *You* have to choose to be happy, by making positive and good choices, doing work on yourself and removing all the blocks and limitations that are preventing you from being happy in the first place.

In the course of my many years of teaching, counseling and advising people, I have found that there are some individuals who will never be happy and it's entirely their choice to live that way.

I also noticed that many people suffer from "If only..." syndrome. This means they walk around saying and thinking, "If I only I had _____, I will be happy". The truth is that happiness is already right in front of you. All you have to do is recognize it, then reach out and give it to yourself like a present. It begins with your understanding that it is not up to other people to make you happy. You will also never have long term happiness as a result of acquiring material possessions. Objects may give you a temporary high or momentary happiness, but that will melt away like a popsicle in the sunshine. It is all temporary.

So, by now you may be wondering what *will* provide you with life-long happiness and daily happiness? What follows is some information on creating your own little happiness bubble; one that you can live in daily and that will help you raise your vibration.

Not too long ago, I took a poll about happiness through my social media accounts to see what my thousands of friends and followers do to have happiness. Here are some of the things they shared, as sources of happiness:

- Good health
- Traveling
- Meditating
- Spending time with family
- Singing and listening to music
- Playing fun games
- Laughing and watching shows that make you laugh
- Making other people smile or laugh
- Spending time outdoors
- Volunteering, helping people or doing service for others (seniors, youth, poor, homeless, etc.)

- Living your purpose
- Spending time with pets or animals
- Playing sports
- Camping
- Fishing
- Doing crafts
- Playing musical instruments
- Dancing
- Building things
- Knitting, sewing, crocheting
- Bird watching
- Hiking
- Gardening – flowers or produce
- Reading books, magazines or blogs
- Going to church or synagogue
- Time with friends
- Meeting new friends
- Shopping
- Exploring
- Visiting museums
- Watching butterflies and dragonflies
- Collecting fairy statues
- Spending time around water (ocean, lake, waterfall)
- Looking at antique or classic cars, trucks, motorcycles

These are just a sample of some of the many answers I received when I did my poll on happiness. I am sure you get the idea by now. Happiness comes not so much from *things*, but from experiences, memories and even spirituality. Happiness comes from going deep within yourself and getting in touch with your higher self, guides, and angels. Happiness especially comes when you connect with God and the Universe and when you recognize your connection to everyone and everything.

If you are a person who regularly uses the words, "*If only I had ___,*" think very deeply about what I just said. Ask yourself and your higher self the question, "*What do I need to do every day to be happy?*" Then, go within yourself, using meditation, quiet time, prayer and reflection and listen for the answers that come up. Take a piece of paper, write down the answers and start doing what makes you happy every day. You already have all the answers within yourself. If you are unhappy right now, here is a new daily mantra for you:

> "I am creating my happiness today and every day."

Say this mantra every day of the week, as many times a day as possible, until you notice a shift towards happiness in your life. Then, start making a conscious choice to be happy. No other person will ever make you happy; only you can do that. If you are still wrestling with unhappiness, maybe you need to lower your expectations and work on removing any upper limits and blocks you have created for yourself.

As the frequency of the Earth is rising, it is becoming easier to quickly manifest things. Every thought, word and action is actually manifesting your reality. You have the ability to manifest a happy life, but you need to be consciously aware of your thoughts, words and actions so that they are focused entirely on what brings you happiness.

I often hear people make comments about other people, saying "Susie will never be happy." There are many reasons why some of the people in our lives will never be happy and the main reason is that they have a false belief about where happiness comes from, in the first place.

Earlier I mentioned having unreasonably high expectations. That's one of the reasons why some people are never happy. However, there are also some people who have the belief that other people, jobs or material things will make them happy or give them long term happiness. Many people suffer from

"If only syndrome." They live their lives eternally saying: *"If only I had a boyfriend, I would be happy;" "If only I had a higher paying job, I would be happy;" "If only I had a Mercedes Benz, I would be happy."*

My personal favorite is *"If only I had a million dollars, I would be happy."*
Unfortunately, the key to happiness is not jobs, other people, money, or material things. According to recent polls, Americans are no happier today than they were 50 years ago despite significant increases in prosperity, decreases in crime, cleaner air, larger living quarters and a better overall quality of life.

"Happiness is 50 percent genetic", says University of Minnesota researcher David Lykken. According to psychologists, the other 50 percent depends on your determination to be happy. Which may be why Abraham Lincoln spoke the words I quoted earlier.
I believe that we are 100% in control of our own happiness and we create our own happiness. I also believe that you *can* get temporary happiness or gratification from things like a new job or money, but you will never receive life-long happiness from those things. Wouldn't it be nice to be happy every day? Well, the truth is that you can be happy every day, if you choose to be!

Earlier in this book I spoke about the fact that happiness is one of the primary purposes of your soul. Every human being shares this purpose and it is our God given right to be happy. Happiness is as important to humans as water, air and food. In fact, if you live in a state of unhappiness every day, you will get sick and die. Unhappiness is basically the same thing as — or part of — overall stress and causes 98% of health problems. You can gauge health by people's level of happiness and being content. Many studies show that people's happiness level is directly tied to their level of wellness and health.

In order to understand how to be happy, you first need to look at the things that keep you from being happy, in the first place. If you are not happy every day, these are some of the many likely reasons why:

- Ego - Negative aspects of your ego (fears, worrying, blame, shame, guilt, hate, jealousy, thinking you are better than others, unforgiveness, malice, rudeness, meanness, condescending behavior, over confidence, laziness, mistrust, lack of tolerance, impatience, and other negative ego issues)
- Stress
- Making bad decisions
- Financial problems or money worries
- Lack of self-love and/or self-respect
- Poor priorities
- Lack of love from others, in your life
- Lack of compassion
- Inability to process, accept and/or express your emotions and feelings
- Lack of gratitude
- Poor health
- Working at a job or career you do not like
- Bad relationships
- Poor communication with people in general
- Poor boundaries or no boundaries
- Unhealed traumas from your childhood or past lifetimes
- Conscious and subconscious blocks to your happiness
- Lack of time management and not enough time to have fun and do what you want
- Not allowing your inner child to come out and play. Basically, your inner child needs healing.
- Not having any fun, including not knowing *how* to have fun

- Mental or physical abuse – either self-abuse or allowing others to abuse you
- Lack of self-care
- Lack of spirituality, disconnect from God and humanity, not understanding oneness, or stuck in duality
- Loneliness
- Boredom

If one or more of these things apply to you, then you are probably not happy every day or you are not as happy as you should be.

As you can see, the first thing on this list — which is the biggest thing that prevents your happiness — is your own ego. Every human on Earth has an Ego. The Ego has been defined in many different ways.

The dictionary defines it as, *"A person's sense of self-esteem or self-importance."*

The Psychoanalysis definition is, *"Ego is the part of the mind that mediates between the conscious and the unconscious and is responsible for reality testing and a sense of personal identity."*

The spiritual definition of ego, according to www.spiritualresearchfoundation.org, is *"Ego means considering oneself to be distinct from others and God due to identification with the physical body and impressions in various centers of the subtle body. In short ego is leading our life as per the thinking that our existence is limited to our 5 senses, mind, and intellect and identifying with them to various degrees."* If you practice spirituality it decreases Ego.

The truth is that Ego is a necessary thing for every human on Earth for both individual identity and personality, as well as for survival. Without Ego people would never aspire to be anything or make anything of themselves. People would not be able to work their way up the ladder in a company or be

168

successful in business or leadership. People would not be driven to accomplish great things.

If everyone on the planet had no Ego at all, there would be no individuality and creativity. Things would not get invented and projects would not be completed because there would not be a desire to pursue better and bigger things nor to invent new ways of doing things. Everything would be status quo, and nothing would change. Everyone would be too similar and life as we know it would be super boring.

However, even though it's important for everyone on Earth to have *some* Ego, not all of Ego is positive. There are good qualities of Ego and bad qualities of Ego. In fact, everything in life and on Earth needs to be in balance and that includes the Ego. If you have too much or too little Ego it can have harmful effects on your body, mind, spirit, life and relationships. According to spirituality, the more you identify with Ego and remain in Ego, the less you identify with and relate to God. The less you identify with and remain in Ego, the closer you identify with God.

As you are reading this book, please ponder this question: "*Is my Ego causing me stress and preventing my happiness?*" Here is why this is important. There are good and bad sides to Ego and all Ego translates to conscious and subconscious thoughts. Negative thoughts — regardless of whether they are conscious or just subconscious tapes playing in the background of your mind — will cause you stress and unhappiness. Negative thoughts also lower your energetic vibrational frequency and harm your energy field on a Quantum Physics level.

There are many negative aspects of the Ego that humans experience daily. I have mentioned these negative aspects earlier in this book. Some of these also manifest as emotions and feelings but they ultimately come from the ego and include things like fears, blame, shame, regrets, jealousy, competition, wanting for things that you cannot ever have, judging other people, criticizing others, boastfulness, bragging, gossiping, possessiveness, high or unreal expectations, insecurity, overly dramatic, holding onto grudges, unwillingness to forgive, too little confidence, too much confidence, greed, boastfulness, gloating, selfishness, lack of patience, believing you are always right, being a know-it-all, beliefs that you are better or more important than others and much more.

These negative aspects of Ego cause unhappiness for you and the other people who are on the receiving end of them. It is impossible to hold a grudge and experience happiness at the same time. It is impossible to be jealous and feel happy at the same time. It is also not possible to do any of the things I mentioned and simultaneously remain happy.

See where I am going with this? Every time you allow yourself to experience these negative aspects of Ego, you are preventing yourself from being happy. True happiness can only be achieved when Ego has been completely diminished to a positive and healthy level. The Buddhist religion and the practice of Mindfulness focus on diminishing the Ego. Negative thoughts and aspects of Ego also cause you to pull farther away from God. The Holy Bible states that "*Every time you judge, you condemn yourself*". It also says "*Guilt and/or shame will draw you further away from the Lord deeper into sin.*" These concepts have been taught not only in Christianity but in many other ancient world religions.

When you have too much Ego or remain in negative Ego, you are also causing stress in your body, mind and spirit, in your relationships and to people around you. If you are wondering how these negative aspects of ego are causing stress, here are some examples.

When you are in negative Ego, meaning that you are being jealous, possessive, judgmental, etc., it harms your relationships and causes unhappiness. Negative Ego also stresses your relationship with God, since God is only unconditional love and does not have any of these human aspects of Ego. Your body and brain experience stress from negative aspects of Ego because every time you think a negative thought It stresses your body and brain by releasing the cortisol stress hormone into your body which can cause disease and health problems.

As I said before, over 98% of illness is caused by stress we create with our own negative emotions, thoughts, feelings and Ego. The negative thoughts harm and impact every cell in your body and even your DNA. These negative thoughts, feelings and emotions also vibrate at a very low frequency, according to Quantum Physics. This low vibration creates health problems and stress in the body, brain and spirit. When you speak negative language to others — which emanates from the negative aspects of your Ego — you are harming the people you are speaking to.

In the Holy Bible there is a story of Jesus cursing a fig tree and then the tree shrivels up and dies *(Matthew 21:18–22; Mark 11:12–14, 20–25)*. This is a lesson that teaches you that words can harm others and your speech is more powerful than your thoughts. Words are spells, hence the term spelling.

If you want to be happy every day of your life and you want to avoid stress, you will have to learn how to diminish your Ego; mainly the negative parts of your Ego that cause the unhappiness and stress I have discussed so far. You will need to learn how to bring your Ego into a balanced and healthy state. Here are some ways that you can do that.

1. Be willing to be 100% truthful and honest with yourself about what negative aspects of Ego you possess or are a problem for you. On a piece of paper draw a line down the middle and write down the negative aspects of your ego on one side of the line. On the other side write down all of the positive parts of your ego like respect, motivation, assertiveness, curiosity and more. This will help you to understand how much work you will need to do to dissolve the negative aspects of Ego. Your goal is to eventually

eliminate all the negative aspects of Ego and be left with only the aspects of Ego that are important to your life and happiness.

2. Learn how to reprogram your mind, thoughts, emotions, and feelings for only positive. In psychology, this is called cognitive behavioral therapy. Cognitive behavioral therapy is also a great way to get rid of anxiety and some forms of depression. Start paying attention to every feeling and thought you have and write them down in a journal. Make particular note of how often you are experiencing the negative ones and start focusing on more positive thoughts, feelings and emotions instead.

3. Practice spirituality, which is the key to diminishing the Ego. Spirituality and religion are two different things. Spirituality is your personal daily practice, focus, intention, rituals and activities that draw you closer to your creator (God). This will be different for every person, but you do not have to be in a church or synagogue to be spiritual.

4. Learn how to meditate daily. There are 108 types of meditation and they include prayer, walking meditations, sitting practices that include Prayer, Bible meditation, Music/sound meditation, QiGong, Mindfulness, Zen, Loving Kindness, Chakra Meditation, Transcendental Meditation, Yoga meditation, Chanting Meditation, Pranayamas, Theta meditation, Breathing, Mantra Meditation, dance meditation, drumming and many more. Meditation opens up your crown chakra and 3rd eye and connects you more closely to creator and helps you diminish ego. Meditation offers hundreds of benefits to your body, mind, spirit, life, relationships, career, etc.

5. Practice gratitude every day. Say a gratitude prayer, go over a list in your head or on paper each day of what you are grateful for. Gratitude not only dissolves the negative aspects of Ego but also creates lasting happiness.

6. Work with a life coach, counselor, healer or mental health practitioner to tackle the negative aspects of your ego and dissolve them.

7. Learn how to practice Mindfulness (present moment awareness). It is very hard to be in Ego, or in negative Ego, if you are constantly focusing on what is happening now. I mentioned before that I became a Certified Mindfulness instructor because the practice of Mindfulness improved every aspect of my life and cured me from an anxiety disorder.

The most important thing to know is that as long as you are experiencing and putting out into the world the negative aspects of Ego, you cannot be happy and enjoy lasting happiness. You will also be stressed.

Also, please understand that you are 100% human which means you will never be perfect, and you are going to make mistakes. And that's okay!!!

Be willing to accept all aspects of your personality and your Ego, forgive yourself and love yourself unconditionally the way God loves you. God created Ego, both the negative and the positive, so that we can have these learning experiences here on Earth. This Earth is a big classroom and without Ego you cannot learn, so don't try to make your Ego *disappear,* and don't judge yourself by your ego. You will never be judged by the unconditionally loving Creator who made you.

It is super important for me to point out that not everyone can be happy all the time. You are going to experience negative events, relationship trials, and many other negative things will happen in your lifetime. It will not be perfect every single day of your life. Happiness takes work; however, you should be able to have one or more happy moments every day. Here are some steps for creating happiness:

- Spend time every day doing something that is fun for you and makes you feel happy. No one else can determine what this is, except for you.
- Find happiness in the little things in life like watching a butterfly or the birds, watching your child play piano, eating a piece of chocolate, having a picnic, buying some flowers and similar things.
- Practice gratitude - focus on what you are grateful for. Keep a journal, say gratitude prayers, or meditate on that for which you are grateful.
- Surround yourself with plants and plant a garden. Some people find great happiness in gardening.
- Take regular vacations
- Go on a camping trip
- Take a walk on the beach, build a sandcastle, go seashell, sea glass or rock hunting, or fly a kite.
- Go for a swim
- Think positive thoughts (accentuate the positive and eliminate the negative)
- Spend quality time with friends and family
- Practice meditation and mindfulness
- Engage in singing, playing or listening to music
- Play fun games or sports
- Laugh and/or watch shows that make you laugh, or make other people smile or laugh
- Spend time in nature
- Volunteer; doing service for others (seniors, youth, poor and etc), practice random acts of kindness
- Spend time with pets or animals
- Do crafts and pursue hobbies
- Dance (Dance like no one is watching)
- Read books, magazines, or blogs

- Attend a church, synagogue, mosque or temple
- Spend time around water (ocean, lake, waterfall)
- Have sex with your partner
- Surround yourself with bright colors – color therapy is great for happiness
- Use aromatherapy – nice fragrances create happiness

One of the best ways you can create happiness for yourself is to engage your inner child. Many people miss out on a good childhood due to lack of parents, poverty, bad parents, abuse, divorce, addictions and many other reasons. As you do your inner child healing work, think about what made you happy when you were a child and do that from time to time. Whether it is going roller skating, blowing bubbles, swinging on a play set, ziplining, hopscotch, riding a roller coaster, dancing like nobody is watching, singing karaoke or playing air hockey, try to pick a thing or two to do for fun once in a while that will engage your inner child. Let your hair down and be a goofball. Do not judge yourself and don't let anyone else judge you, either.

Don't worry! Be happy!

Chapter 15

Creating Your Own Personal Ascension Roadmap

We came here to Earth to forget who we are, but now it's time to remember.

You are on your way down the road to remembering who you are. Some of you may remember more than others, but now is the time to create your own personal roadmap for your Ascension, so that when you leave this Earth you have absolutely no regrets.

When I leave here I want to be able to say "*I accomplished everything I came here for; I now know exactly who I am, everywhere I have been before this life and where I am going on my journey; I reclaimed my sovereignty, I did as many things as I could that were important for my soul learning, I made a positive impact on as many people as I could, I helped every person and animal that I could; I was a good mother, father, husband, wife, sister, brother and friend, I created a legacy of love, compassion and kindness; I shined my light brightly and I assisted Mother Gaia in the return of Christ Consciousness.*"

I pray that after reading this book and assimilating and absorbing this information — which was mostly channeled from Yeshua — you will have some basic skills and the knowledge to accomplish everything you came here to Earth for, to embrace your sovereignty, complete your Ascension with love and happiness and get to know the powerful divine being that is you.

It is time for you to create a roadmap for own Ascension process. Now that you have read this guidebook, it will be beneficial for you to create this roadmap by making some lists of what you will need for your Ascension journey.

- Make a list of all the things you need to do; that you have not already done.
- Make a list of all the tools you need to purchase for your journey and purchase them. For example: tuning forks, singing bowls, crystals and stones, essential oils, protection devices for electronics and home, spiritual books, and anything else you need to assist you with the journey.
- Make a list of any services you need to help you, such as having a private session with me or an energy healer, shaman or other practitioner.
- Make a list of things in your life that you need to clear, heal, work on and improve. Make sure to prioritize everything in order of importance.
- Follow the signs that you are on the right road when they present themselves – angel numbers like 1111,1212, 222, 333, 555, etc.; synchronicities, people, messages, events, visions, feelings, emotions, dreams, intuition, downloads, channeled messages, new abilities, receiving prosperity, healing evidence, meeting people who are important for your journey, etc.
- Keep a journal to take notes on everything you are doing and to track all the changes taking place in your life.
- Be compassionate and loving with yourself throughout this whole process. Ascension is not a competition, you are not on a time schedule, you are not broken but you are not perfect, you are an eternal spiritual being having a human experience.

I hope this book has been helpful for you, resonated with your energy and higher self, and I hope that you learned at least one new idea.

This information I have presented is just a basic road map for you to get started on your own personal journey of Ascension. Now its up to you to decide which roads you take, how much time you spend on each, what to study, and learn next, etc. Your path will continue to get clearer the longer you are on it.

If you have more spiritual, esoteric or metaphysical questions, and you're interested in having a private session with me, want to sign up for one of my classes, wish for me come speak at your conference or retreat, or you are interested in collaborating with me to co-create our new 5D heavenly Earth, please contact me through my website:

www.spiritualgrowthjourneys.com

Appendix 1

Recommended reading

During my entire life I have been reading books and always wanted to learn as much as I possibly could in this lifetime. There is an overwhelming number of spiritual books out there, so you need to be discerning with your choices. Here are some of my personal favorite spiritual books that may be helpful for you on your Ascension journey.

- Any books by Dolores Cannon
- "The Law of One" series by Don Elkins
- "The Urantia Book" by the Urantia Foundation
- "The 'I AM' Discourses" by Ascended Master St. Germain
- "The Sophia Code" by Kai Ra
- "The Ascension Mysteries" by David Wilcock
- "The Afterlife Interviews" by Jeffrey A. Marks.
- "The Power of Awareness" by Neville Goddard.
- "The Art of Happiness" by His Holiness the Dalai Lama.
- "The Four Agreements" by Don Miguel Ruiz
- "You can Heal Your Life" by Louise Hay
- "Heal Your Body" by Louise Hay
- "Living the Wisdom of the Tao" by Dr. Wayne Dyer

To assist you in starting an effective meditation practice, I highly recommend reading
"The Miracle of Mindfulness: An Introduction to the Practice of Meditation" by Thich Nhat Hanh; Mobi Ho (Translator),

For emotional healing, stress and similar topics: "The Biology of Belief" by Dr. Bruce H. Lipton PhD

To learn more about the quantum energy field: Any books by Gregg Braden,

"E Squared" by Pam Grout

For sound healing music: Any CD by Jonathan Goldman

About the Author

Kimberly Palm is a Spiritual Teacher and Ascension Guide for awake souls seeking the truth on their journey.

She lives in the Pacific Northwest of the United States with her husband and two children. Kimberly has been spiritually mentoring people since she was a teenager because of her special abilities and her love for helping people.

Kimberly has studied metaphysics, spirituality, esoterics, world religion, energy healing and holistic health for most of her life. She uses her knowledge and experience as well as her special gifts, including intuition, clairvoyance, channeling, energy skills, empathic abilities and more, to guide people on their spiritual journey. Kimberly enjoys teaching people how to use their own inner compass, find their own truth, and she especially enjoys answering her clients esoteric and spiritual questions.

Kimberly has been speaking and teaching on various subjects since 1990. To book a private session with Kimberly, contact her for a speaking engagement, collaboration, or to sign up for Kimberly's classes, please visit her website www.spiritualgrowthjourneys.com

Made in the USA
Coppell, TX
22 November 2020

41872244R00101